MW00988633

Psalms as a Grammar for Faith

Psalms as a Grammar for Faith

Prayer and Praise

W. H. Bellinger Jr.

BAYLOR UNIVERSITY PRESS

© 2019 by Baylor University Press
Waco, Texas 76798

Cover Design by Savanah N. Landerholm
Cover image: Section from the Psalms Scrolls, Qumran cave 11, c.30-50 (parchment) / The Israel Museum, Jerusalem, Israel / Bridgeman Images
Book Design by Savanah N. Landerholm

The Library of Congress has cataloged this book under ISBN 978-1-4813-1118-2.

Printed in the United States of America on acid-free paper with a minimum of thirty percent recycled content.

FOR LIBBY

CONTENTS

ACKNOWLEDGMENTS

It takes a village to produce a book. I express profound thanks to a number of people. I have learned much from many Psalms scholars and especially thank those associated with the Society of Biblical Literature. My Old Testament colleagues at Baylor University contribute remarkably to our scholarly mission. I have learned much from graduate students through the years. I am grateful to the Baylor University Department of Religion faculty and staff, the Baylor College of Arts and Sciences and its deans, and the provost and president of the university for a context in which to thrive as a scholar and teacher. I am grateful to work in a setting that encourages rigorous scholarship and commitment to communities of faith. Graduate students Rebecca Poe Hays, Lacy Crocker Papadakis, and Chwi-Woon Kim have provided much assistance with the book project. Mr. Kim has been especially helpful in producing the final form of the volume. I had the opportunity to explore some of the topics in the first three chapters in lectures at the Campbell University Divinity School in North Carolina and at George W. Truett Theological Seminary at Baylor and at Westover Hills Presbyterian Church in Little Rock, Arkansas. I also thank greatly Dr. Carey Newman and the outstanding publishing team at Baylor University Press. I owe a debt of gratitude to many.

I have worked on the Psalms for decades and written about this beautiful text in various forms. This volume explores a contemporary reading of the Psalms in the form-critical tradition in which I have been educated but accounting for recent scholarly developments. The volume also explores facets of the shape and shaping of the Hebrew Psalter as a whole, a more recent direction in Psalms scholarship. The goal of this modest volume is to help students and clergy interpret the Psalms with deep meaning and to appropriate deeply these profound poetic texts. Some recent Psalms studies have worked on the Septuagint and on the Qumran materials of the Psalms. I have limited this study to the Hebrew Psalter.

I dedicate the book to my wife Libby who, because of my research, has lived with the Psalms longer than she could imagine!

W. H. Bellinger Jr.

Advent 2018

THE BOOK OF PSALMS

READING THE PSALMS TODAY

Often when people of faith gather around the Hebrew Scriptures, the focus is the book of Psalms, but I wonder if such gatherings pause to think about why we study the Psalms and why these texts continue to be so important for a great variety of readers. Certainly one reason we read the Psalms is that we follow the tradition of those who came before us. These texts have powerfully influenced worship and theology, ethics and piety for centuries and continue to do so today. A brief look at history will help us to see the import of the book of Psalms.

A RICH TRADITION OF READING

Jewish and Christian worshipers and readers have found much in the Psalms throughout history. William L. Holladay and Susan E. Gillingham have provided us with helpful recent accounts of this reception history of the Psalms.[1] It begins even before the close of the Hebrew canon and continues until today.

Jewish Readings

The Qumran community that produced the Dead Sea Scrolls cited both canonical and noncanonical psalms and used them in worship.[2] The Mishnah cites a number of psalms and gives instructions for reciting them in daily

life and on specific occasions.[3] Jewish tradition continued to emphasize the
Psalms with, for example, Saadiah Gaon (882–942 CE) characterizing the
Psalms as a second Torah; Abraham ibn Ezra (1089–1164 CE) emphasizing
their aesthetic quality; and David Kimchi using the Psalms to refute Christian views.[4]

The Psalms continue to play a central part in Jewish liturgy. Most of the
psalms used come from the categories of praise and thanksgiving. While Pss
6 and 137 are important in the liturgy, lament psalms are not strongly represented.[5] The Psalms have also been important in Jewish music, architecture,
and art. Music marking the founding of the modern state of Israel included
works based on various texts in the book of Psalms.[6] Jewish tradition has
often associated Pss 22 and 44 with the Holocaust.[7]

Christian Readings

Early Church. The New Testament often depicts Jesus, the disciples, and early
Christians singing psalms in worship contexts (Matt 26:30; Mark 14:26;
Acts 4:24; 1 Cor 14:26; Eph 5:19; Col 3:16). There is wide consensus that the
Psalms are the book from the Older Testament most often quoted by New
Testament writers. The early church fathers and mothers loved the Psalms.
For example, Athanasius wrote in his *Letter to Marcellinus,*

> And the one who hears is deeply moved, as though he himself were speaking, and
> is affected by the words of the songs, as if they were his own songs . . . . And it
> seems to me that these words become like a mirror to the persons singing them,
> so that he might perceive himself and the emotions of his soul, and thus affected
> he might recite them.[8]

Augustine in the fourth century CE said, "What utterances sent I unto thee,
my God, when I read the Psalms, those faithful songs and sounds of devotion. . . . What utterances I used to send up unto thee in those Psalms, and
how was I inflamed toward thee by them."[9] The Psalms took prominent roles
in the liturgy of the church both West and East. Singing and reciting psalms
are long-standing traditions in monastic communities, especially those
that follow the Benedictine Rule. Most monastic communities followed the
Benedictine Rule in the seventh through the eleventh centuries. Illuminated
Psalters also reflect an aesthetic appreciation of the Psalms from this time.

Medieval Era. Monastic communities continued to use the whole Psalter
in the Medieval Era. Because of the widespread use of the Psalms in both
private and corporate settings, the Psalter was "perceived to be the property
of lay Christians in a way that the rest of the Scriptures were not."[10] The

Psalms were also used for teaching in primary education, and both Langland's *Piers Plowman* (c. 1377) and Chaucer's *Canterbury Tales* (1387–1400) made frequent use of the Psalms.[11] Illuminated Psalters remained popular, and illustrations from psalms began to appear in stained-glass windows in cathedrals and abbeys.[12] The Psalms were very much part of everyday life.

Reformation Era. The Psalms were also favored by the Protestant Reformers. Martin Luther translated the Psalms from the Hebrew and encouraged the reading of the whole Psalter in worship.[13] Several of Luther's hymns such as "A Mighty Fortress" were based on the Psalms. He labeled the book the "Little Bible" because it encapsulates so much of the message of the Scriptures. He also emphasized that the Psalms, even though they originated from centuries ago, seem to fit the occasions in which contemporary people pray, as if they were written for just that person in just that circumstance.[14]

John Calvin called the Psalms the anatomy of all the parts of the human soul.[15] It seems that Calvin very much identified with the Davidic experience reflected in the Psalms.[16] Calvin published metrical Psalters. The Calvinist tradition was a major force in bringing the singing of psalms into congregational worship as well as the appropriation of the Psalms for daily life.[17] In a preface to the 1542 Geneva Psalter, Calvin wrote:

> Now what Saint Augustine says is true, that no one is able to sing things worthy of God unless he has received them from him. Wherefore, when we have looked thoroughly everywhere and searched high and low, we shall find no better songs nor more appropriate for the purpose than the Psalms . . . And furthermore, when we sing them we are certain that God puts the words in our mouths, as if he himself were singing in us to exalt his glory.[18]

Reformation Era–women such as Katharina Schütz Zell from Strasbourg and Justitia Sanger from Braunschweig also published commentaries on various psalms, and a number of hymns from this era drew from the Psalms.[19]

Roman Catholic Tradition. While the use of the Psalms in Roman Catholicism remained relatively constant during the Reformation Era, new music settings of the texts emerged, and the Psalms eventually became a greater part of the Mass.[20] Dorothy Day spoke of how important the Psalms were to her while protesting in the women's suffrage movement: "I read [the Bible] with the sense of coming back to something of my childhood that I had lost. My heart swelled with joy and thankfulness for the Psalms. The man who sang these songs knew sorrow and expected joy."[21] Thomas Merton encouraged all Christians to pray the Psalms:

No one can doubt that the Church considers the Psalms the ideal prayer for her clerics and religious. They form the largest part of the divine office. But the main purpose of this short essay is to remind the reader that the Psalter is also a perfect form of prayer for the layman.[22]

Recent Times. The Psalms have continued to be popular around the world and in various quarters of Christendom. Much church music continues to reflect these poems, as does liturgy in various Christian traditions. Stained glass and other Christian images continue to invoke the Psalms.[23] Dietrich Bonhoeffer found great courage and faith in the Psalms during his imprisonment in Nazi Germany.[24] He speaks of the Psalms as where the God who is concealed in the world is revealed. G. Henton Davies, the Baptist scholar from Oxford of a generation past, would ask the question, "Why do we study the Psalms?" And he would answer that ancient Israel knew how to come into the presence of God and they knew how to behave when they got there! Today Ps 23 continues as an icon of faith for many,[25] and Ps 100 calls many congregations to worship. The Psalms are the most read of all the books of the Older Testament because they powerfully shape faith and the life of faith by shaping the encounter with the living God. Gillingham notes the key role of the Psalter in ecumenical and interfaith dialogues during the last hundred years. She argues that "this is because the Psalter, more than any other part of the Bible, represents a common tradition of prayer and praise to the same God" in a society where religious belief has declined.[26]

There are, of course, many other literary uses of the Psalms—in Shakespeare and in many English poems and hymns. This survey suggests that we study the Psalms because of the long history of their usage in religious practice and because their profound impact on the life of faith is currently experienced by many. In this chapter, I want to put that reality in a slightly different way. I want to suggest that the Psalms provide us with a grammar of faith, a means of expressing a vibrant relationship with God. In chapters 2 and 3, I want to explore two main dimensions of that grammar of faith—prayer and praise.

But in this introductory essay, I need to reflect more broadly on reading the Psalms as this grammar of faith. That is so because while many read the Psalms devotionally or in the hospital room or at the graveside or use them in worship, we seldom preach them or teach them. I earlier mentioned Pss 23 and 100; perhaps we could add Ps 46 or a couple of others to a list of psalms used devotionally.[27] I think we use those favorites and know most of the other psalms only in some vague memory that we struggle to access. This point is crucial because if the Psalms are to be a grammar of faith, a resource for faith in both the crises and joys of life and all the times in between, the resource needs to be at the ready. So we need to preach and teach the Psalms in order to provide this resource, this grammar, to ourselves and our congregations for full and faithful living.

Perhaps you know the story Kathleen Norris tells in her memoir *The Cloister Walk*.[28] She had grown up going to church, and faith centered on this time to be fully "dressed up" outside and in to meet God. She understood that she was trying to be good following Christ. It was years later, when she had the opportunity to spend time in a Benedictine community where the Psalms were the focus of worship and were used throughout the day, that she became immersed in these prayed poems and embraced them as a grammar of faith in the highs and lows of life and everything in between. The community moved through the entire Psalter every three or four weeks. The words of the Psalms "washed over" her; the prayer and praise of the Psalms stunningly expressed her true life. She came to address God not "dressed up" but as she was. We will not all have such an opportunity to become a Benedictine oblate, but I hope we can find in our classrooms and congregations contexts and ways for reading and studying the Psalms together so that these texts are woven into the warp and woof of our living. Then, when we come to the joys and the full days and the crises, the words of the Psalms can provide us the grammar to crawl and walk and run in faith, in the tradition of the saints of old, as articulated in the Psalter. I am asking that we add an eleventh commandment: "Thou shalt preach and teach the Psalms." I would characterize the book of Psalms as both the prayer book and the hymnbook of the faith community of ancient Israel—a book that shapes faith and life—and so we need to find ways to explore it in greater depth. The Psalms are both deeply personal and enmeshed in a worshiping community. They relate to all of life. They do not provide comfortable reading in a culture characterized by optimism and its partner, denial. These texts express both pain and its hard-won transformation into praise.[29]

I commend to us all the story of a pastor whose congregation had done such a study, and it made the spiritual resource of the Psalms present when he needed it to deal with a pastoral crisis. A family had lost a three-month-old daughter/granddaughter. The congregation had, among other things, studied and prayed the Psalms in groups and memorized these texts and used them through the year in worship. They had prayed psalms with people in crisis and in joy. They had learned and lived with the Psalms and so had been formed by these ancient true-to-life texts. The pastor led the stunned and grieving family in praying Ps 23 as a prayer for a time when no one knows what to say. This encounter became a time of grace for a family and friend in crisis and for a pastor. The resource of this grammar of faith was at hand because of the congregation's emphasis on the Psalms.[30] Such contemporary narratives call us to explore ever more deeply this grammar of faith we call the Psalter in the rich tradition of reading the Psalms born witness to by the saints who have come before us. We need to hear the Psalms and respond to them and begin to live in them.

A GRAMMAR OF FAITH

A grammar structures a language so that it communicates, typically with words and their relationships. The use of the term "grammar" to articulate matters of faith and theology alludes to Ludwig Wittgenstein's notion of theology as grammar.[31] The full implications of Wittgenstein's comments have been a matter of considerable discussion. He suggests that a grammar serves the purpose of characterizing what is being discussed, and so theology as grammar articulates an understanding of God. There are different kinds of grammar. Paul Holmer has provided one of the helpful explorations of grammar as an expression of faith.[32] He compares grammar as an expression of faith to learning a language until it becomes second nature to communicate in that language, even in the form of singing.[33] One can communicate with a grammar without explicitly listing the rules of the grammar. Holmer also suggests that the grammar of faith can be appropriated in worship in imaginative ways and that believers can enter the grammar and live with it so that it leads to an encounter with God.[34] A grammar is an ideal that expresses the shared intuitions and features and patterns of faith and so what is included in faith.[35] Theology as grammar has to do with the faith formation of persons and how they live. Lives shaped by the grammar of faith reveal God. "As a person's life slowly grows into the demanding usages of the language about God, seeking to conform one's will to what it demands of a human life, one *becomes* like the reality of which it speaks."[36]

Andrew Moore has more recently explored this theme of grammar and faith. He harks back to Wittgenstein in suggesting that grammar provides the means of governing concepts without explicitly stating the rules. The context in which the grammar is used is central to its shaping of the content it expresses. Grammar provides a way to talk and to guide actions and emotions.[37] Moore explores prescriptive and formational understandings of theology as grammar and how this grammar relates to God's involvement in the world and in life.[38]

I also use the understanding of the Psalms as a grammar of faith in the sense articulated by Molly T. Marshall: "The psalms offer us a grammar to speak our faith. Our faith is formed by praying these searching texts. They introduce us to the One before whom all hearts are open; they offer us ways to share life more fully with God."[39] The quote begins her paper's concluding section, "The Psalter as Grammar for Faith." As the worshiping community and its believers pray the Psalms, they articulate their faith, that is, they speak in the grammar of faith the Psalms provide. The grammar articulates the building blocks of faith. I would go further to say that this speaking (or singing!) not only expresses faith but also helps the singers to appropriate the faith and continue to comprehend and live in the faith and to mature in it, to learn it. This grammar for faith can become the grammar *of* faith for believers and communities. Marshall notes that the Psalter's grammar of faith presses issues of theodicy. The lament psalms provide particularly prescient language for the contemporary pilgrimage of faith, as we will see. So I understand the Psalms to articulate/sing faith and make it possible to grow in the faith and live the faith. The Psalms as a grammar of faith also reveal more about the community and people of the faith.[40]

Peter Candler suggests that medieval theologians thought of texts as maps or itineraries through a journey. We can look at maps and see various landmarks indicated. Or we can through focused imagination and memory enter the map and walk along its paths and see in the mind's eye the landmarks and their significance on the way to a destination. "By the arduous act of reading the reader is given a route, with indicative markers and signs, towards a destination," says Candler. Sites plotted on the map become "stations of the way, to be stopped at and stayed in before continuing; or they could serve as route indicators, 'this way' or 'slow down' or 'skim this quickly' or 'note well.'"[41] To enter the map and make the journey becomes the destination—what Candler labels a grammar of participation. The reader engages the text in conversation. The Psalter as grammar of faith and the language of a life engage each other. The grammar forms life.

Critical Study of the Psalms

I will attend to the standard introductory issues about the book of Psalms in the context of strategies for reading these texts today.[42] Let me at this point simply say that the word "psalm" comes from the Greek title of the book and means "song." I will also often use "Psalter," the Latin title, which means the stringed instrument that accompanies the songs. The Hebrew title is *sēper təhillîm*, Book of Praises. The book includes 150 psalms organized in five sections—usually called books—each concluding with a benediction. The language of five books of the book of Psalms gets confusing, and so I will often speak of the five books of the Hebrew Psalter. The fivefold structure is probably a parallel to the Pentateuch—five books of Torah or instruction and five books of psalms in poetic response. Of the 150 psalms, 116 include a superscription, a brief title written above the poem and included in the Hebrew versification. Scholars agree that these superscriptions arose in the process of the formation of the book. These headings at times indicate the collection from which the psalm comes, give instructions for its use in worship, and include some historical notes. The compilers of the Psalter have used various collections and reflect the understanding that these texts are worship texts, though some of the terms that apparently relate to the musical use of the Psalms are obscure. The sparse historical notes in the superscriptions connect psalms to particular life settings. The superscription to Ps 57 includes all of these elements.

> To the Leader: Do Not Destroy (apparently hymn tune for worship). Of David.
> A Miktam (collection), when he fled from Saul, in the cave (historical note).

We will return to these introductory matters, but with these initial comments on what the Psalter is and why we study it, I now want to come to the heart of reading the Psalms today, that is, how we study the Psalms. It will be clear from what I have already said that we are not the first ones to make this journey of exploring the Psalms. The rich history of reading the Psalms recounted above is a considerable gift from which we can learn. The history of scholarship is also a gift from which we can learn—about how to study the Psalms, this powerful grammar of faith.

Form-Critical Studies

Hermann Gunkel. The modern study of the Psalms began in the latter part of the nineteenth century with the work of Hermann Gunkel.[43] Prior to his work, the Psalms were typically studied with a personal/historical approach in which one looked for the setting in a person's life or a historical event in the life of the community as the point of origin and the key for interpretation. A number of scholars came to see, however, that the open poetic language of the Psalms really makes it impossible to decide which person or event necessarily led to the origin of the text. The language of the Psalms is representative or universally applicable, rather than specific to just one person or event. This adaptability for life is a crucial part of the character of the language of these poetic prayers that makes it possible for all of us to pray these texts. Gunkel sought to put Psalms interpretation on a firmer footing by reading with a comparative eye the 150 Psalms and other psalms in the Bible, such as the song of Miriam/Moses in Exod 15 or the Magnificat in Luke 1 and other psalms collected from the cultures surrounding ancient Israel. He considered literary structures, vocabulary, and religious feeling and categorized the Psalms by type or form or genre. This move began the modern form-critical study of the Psalms and profoundly changed the way of reading the Psalms in the scholarship and theology of western culture. It provided a means of organizing one's study and made it possible to study types of psalms together and to study individual psalms in light of those similar to them.

The different types of psalms Gunkel listed can be summed up in the following categories:

- The hymns of praise offer adoration to God as creator and redeemer. They begin by calling the congregation to praise and often conclude with a renewed call to praise. The body of the hymn articulates reasons why the congregation should offer praise to God.
- Individual and community thanksgiving psalms narrate how persons of faith or the community have been delivered from crises in the context of praise and gratitude to the God who delivers. These texts thus offer a particular kind of praise.
- Individual and community laments come from a crisis of persons, such as illness or oppression, or a crisis of the community, such as war or famine. These prayers address Israel's God and portray the crisis and call for help. They usually come to a positive conclusion.
- The royal psalms come from various events in the life of the Davidic king in Jerusalem, such as battle or a royal coronation. This category relates more to that royal setting than to literary characteristics.
- Wisdom poems derive from the wisdom teachers in ancient Israel and reflect the perspectives of the books usually classified as wisdom literature, especially the book of Proverbs.

What Gunkel found was that the psalms of praise and the prayers for help typically have a common structure; attention to those patterns of the psalms can provide helpful guides for reading these texts and for embracing their power. The second part of Gunkel's approach was to ask in what setting in ancient Israel's social and religious life these psalm types originated, and his answer was that they came from worship.

Sigmund Mowinckel. It was Gunkel's student Sigmund Mowinckel who pursued this insight to its full extent.[44] It is not only that we have various types of psalms, but also that these very psalms come from the actual vibrant worship of the ancient faith community, not exclusively but primarily at the temple in Jerusalem. The import of Mowinckel's study of the Psalms in worship is crucial when we read them. When we read, "Make a joyful noise to the Lord, all the earth. Worship the Lord with gladness; come into his presence with singing" (Ps 100), we are not talking about sitting and thinking that it will be good to praise God. We are reading the script for a community literally to process into the sanctuary while singing. Psalm 26:6-7 talks about washing "my hands in innocence" and going "around the altar" singing songs of thanksgiving that tell of God's "wondrous deeds." The Psalms are about real acts of worship that express the relationship between God and congregation in word and deed. That was the focus of ancient Israel's regular and festival worship, worship that envisioned the world of the creator and redeemer and life in that world. With such a vision, the community of faith was called to sing a new song for the God of *ḥesed we'emet*, the God of persistent love and fidelity, as the God who reigns in this world. Such worship renews the community for full and faithful living.

So I am suggesting that we read the Psalms today first by asking not who wrote the text when or out of what historical event, but that we ask what type and structure of psalm we are reading and how it might relate to ancient Israel's worship, Mowinckel's cult-functional method. I think we do some of those things intuitively when we see the worship language of the Psalms and we see their movement and how they are alike and different, but I also think many of us continue to romanticize the Psalms. We tie them to the singer-shepherd David and think of them in terms of a kind of private piety and devotion on a hillside and of David with a harp singing to beautifully idealized sheep in a romanticized painting. Let me be clear. The Psalms may well be the most significant texts of piety and devotion anywhere, but reading them in sweet, idealized ways perverts their very words and removes them from the real life of faith lived today. Careful reading of the various types of psalms with their literary patterns and attending to their connection with worship can help us avoid such sinful corruption.

David and the Psalms. With that, I should pause and say a word about David and the Psalms. David is often portrayed as the sweet singer of psalms and even as the author of the Psalter. His name does appear in a majority of the superscriptions. The name appears with a Hebrew preposition *lāmed*—so *lə-dāwid*—that has been interpreted in terms of authorship, but it more likely means, among other things, "for David" or "to David" or "belonging to David." Given the use of such terms in various superscriptions, the most likely interpretation is that the term lists the collection from which the psalm comes, the Davidic hymnbook that carries the royal sanction for use in worship in the Jerusalem temple. David is associated with psalmody and may well have written psalms, but I think the best way to think about David and the book of Psalms is that he was the patron of psalmody in ancient Israel and the one who authorized the use of psalms in worship in Jerusalem. A few superscriptions also allude to narratives in the life of David. Interestingly, in all of them, David is not the grand and glorious king but the person of faith who is in great need, whether fleeing from Saul, who is controlled by enmity, or facing Philistine opponents. These allusions suggest that we read these psalms along with the relevant narratives in David's story as a way of seeing the prayers used in a real-life circumstance of a person of faith at prayer in the midst of crisis.[45] So David's connection to the Psalms is strong and important. It is a connection of worship and of the honest dialogue of faith in the midst of real life.

The historical narratives in the psalm superscriptions provide a hermeneutical clue from the scribes who collected these texts. They suggest three emphases: that readers of these psalms consider the texts in tandem with the narratives alluded to in the books of Samuel, that central to the portrayal of the character David is a transparent piety, and that these prayers related to settings in real pilgrimages of faith.

The Davidic psalms are not the only collection in the Psalter. The Korahite and Asaphite collections are also included along with the Psalms of Ascents in Pss 120–134.[46] The Hebrew Psalter is a collection of collections. The fact that the Elohistic Psalter (Pss 42–83) includes psalms from both Korahite and Asaphite collections reflects the process of compilation. We do not know the complete story of how these collections came together, but perhaps the Korahite and Asaphite collections were added to the core Davidic collections, bringing community emphases to the individual prayers in the Davidic psalms. Further psalms that emphasize the reign of God were added, and the collection moved toward the full praise of God in its final stages of compilation. This purposeful process of bringing together the book of Psalms reflects the community's articulation of faith in terms of prayer and praise.

Walter Brueggemann. Let me come at the broader issue in another way. In 1980, Walter Brueggemann powerfully entered the conversation on classifying the Psalms by type. He suggested a different kind of typology tied to lived faith. His types are psalms of orientation, disorientation, and new orientation. He suggests that the Psalter begins with orientation, the guaranteed order of the creation seen in the clear distinctions and places in life for the righteous and the wicked in Ps 1. But the pattern of life suggested further in the Psalms makes clear that suffering comes and the guarantee fades, and disorientation asserts itself in the songs of disarray, the lament psalms. Psalm 6 illustrates with a prayer in the midst of terror but also with a move toward hope. This surprise move toward hope brings a new orientation expressed in the songs of new life, comprising thanksgiving psalms and some hymns of praise. This new orientation is not the old jaded guarantee but a new way forward with lessons from the experience of disorientation taken into account.[47] There is the sense of crucifixion and resurrection in this pattern. Brueggemann's categories of psalms of orientation, disorientation, and new orientation relate immediately to the life of faith and to social settings present in a variety of cultural contexts and so have been influential with church groups study-ing the Psalms. Any typology seeks to give readers structures to begin their reading and interpretation, and his is no different. What is different is the kinds of types used for the categorization. His types have to do with lived faith experience rather than literary or historical categories. Brueggemann's typology is different from Gunkel's, but both remind us of the variety in the kinds of psalms and nudge us toward realizing that the Psalms are not private or syrupy but public and relational. They get to the deep-down stuff of faith. They provide us with the words and grammar of worship and faith, a powerful and well-seasoned grammar for all of life.

The Shape and Shaping of the Psalter

So I have suggested that part of reading the Psalms today has to do with the various types of psalms and their connection to worship, but there is more. Gerald Wilson, a good Baylor graduate, published a book in 1985 that suggests that when we read psalms, we need to think about their context in the book of Psalms as a whole.[48] Most of us read the Psalms as discrete poems. We read Ps 23 and do not think about its connections to Ps 22 or Ps 24 or where it falls in the Hebrew Psalter. We have seen that the Hebrew Psalter is a collection of collections. The Davidic collections are the most prominent, but there are also, among others, Korahite and Asaphite collections, apparently from guilds of temple worship leaders, and the Songs of Ascents, a collection of pilgrimage songs in Pss 120–134. The collections exhibit characteristics that can help in reading the texts they include. The Psalter was apparently put together by collections, with the Davidic psalms at the core. Then the psalms of the Korahites and of Asaph come into the picture, and eventually

Books I–III come together. Wilson has shown that Books I–III, Pss 1–89, have a different editorial history than do Books IV–V, Pss 90–150.[49] With these latter books, psalms of the community and psalms of praise become more prominent. Most Psalms scholars today would agree that there is a shape to the Hebrew Psalter, and so I suggest that a third question to ask in reading psalms today is where the psalm appears in the Hebrew Psalter.[50] The three questions, then, are the psalm's genre (and structure), the psalm's connection to worship, and the psalm's location in the Hebrew Psalter.

Not all scholars agree with Wilson's account of the shape and shaping of the Hebrew Psalter. Jerome Creach proposes an emphasis on the destiny of the righteous as the focus of the movement of the book.[51] Some would suggest that the figure of David comes back into view in the latter books of the Psalter and argue that Wilson does not account for that literary fact. Was the community that shaped the Psalter looking for a return of the Davidic kingdom or some kind of eschatological hope?[52] In a recent volume, Michael Snearly has argued that the purposeful arrangement of Book V of the Psalter "signals a renewed hope in the royal/Davidic promises" and so lends an eschatological perspective to the shape of the book as a whole.[53] Not all the issues related to the shape and shaping of the Hebrew Psalter are settled, but this question is now clearly important in the study of the book of Psalms.

Consider this context for the book as a whole. Psalms 1 and 2 serve introductory purposes, and then the narrative moves to persistent prayers for divine help from individuals in crises that involve enemies. With the move to Book III in Ps 73, it becomes clear that the suffering, the disorientation, the power of death, come to the fore for both individuals and the community, especially seen in the crisis of the fall of Jerusalem in the sixth century BCE and the onset of the Babylonian exile. The beginning of the Psalter in Ps 2 saw the celebration of the Davidic kingdom; by the end of Book III, that kingdom is no more and the question to YHWH has become, "Where is that steadfast love and faithfulness of which the community has been singing?" Very quickly in Book IV the story of the Psalter moves back to a time before David to celebrate, beginning in Ps 93, the kingship of YHWH. What will the community do now that the kingdom of David has fallen? Ancient Israel will remember the transforming reality that long before there was a David, the community had a ruler, the living God YHWH, the creator who reigns and who redeems and who guides. That is how this community will live into the future beyond the disaster of exile and its aftermath. The congregation will sing together on the pilgrimage of faith, journeying toward the true worship of YHWH, who redeems and blesses and guides. Ancient Israel will remember and experience again the mighty acts of God and the mighty presence of God and the mighty words of God that renew for life. The community will pray and sing of the God who reigns even in the midst of exile and trouble and woe. The fourth and lengthy fifth book of Psalms lead to the fivefold doxological conclusion of full-throated, uninhibited praise of God in Pss 146–150 and the final words in the great symphony of the extensive call to praise that is Ps 150: "Let everything that breathes praise the Lord! Praise the Lord!"

That account of the shape of the Hebrew Psalter informs its grammar of faith, which contemporary people of faith can sing and live. It is indeed powerfully transforming. My point here is that when we read the Psalms today, the best stewardship of that opportunity to study them includes the question of where this particular psalm comes in that story crafted for us in the Hebrew Psalter. For example, when we read the questioning reflection about the justice of life in Ps 73, what does it matter that this text comes at the beginning of Book III? The psalm is at the beginning of the Psalms of Asaph and marks a turning point in the Hebrew Psalter. It follows a plethora of individual laments that raise a number of theodical questions. The psalm's concluding verses take a theocentric view of these questions and begin to move readers to the questions of the community's suffering that follow in the remainder of Book III and lead to the collection of psalms in Book IV that celebrate the reign of YHWH. What about the praise of God in Ps 100? How does it relate to Book IV? It serves as the benediction concluding the collection of YHWH mālāk (reigns) psalms. Such a concluding song of praise seems to have been customary for psalm collections. Another example is how individual prayers for help often conclude with an emphasis on the community. Psalm 130 provides a word of hope for the community at the conclusion of an individual prayer. Psalm 22 applies an individual's prayer for help to the community's suffering, perhaps in exile. We have already noted that Pss 1 and 2 play significant interpretive roles as texts that introduce the Hebrew Psalter. We have also noted the importance of Psalms 146–150 as the fivefold doxology of praise concluding the book. The literary placement of these texts holds import both for the interpretation of the Psalter as a whole and for each of those individual psalms. You may think these questions are but the obscure musings of an old academic, but they are at the heart of the grammar of faith that is the book of Psalms. So when we read the Psalms today as faithful ministers of the gospel, I suggest we attend to the various types of psalms, their connections to worship, and their place in the Hebrew Psalter as a whole. The last concern moves the question of setting from setting in ancient Israel's social and religious life to literary setting in the book of Psalms. But there is yet more!

HEBREW POETRY

The other important issue in reading the Psalms concerns its poetic language. How Hebrew poetry works is rather different from traditional English poetry, with its sound rhyme. It is basic to remember that Hebrew poetry typically centers on parallel structures—parallel words, parallel lines, parallel stanzas. Echo effects are central to the poetry: "The LORD watches over the way of the righteous but (yes, and even more so in contrast) the way of the wicked will perish" (Ps 1:6). This poetic parallelism often gets translated into English. But there is more than parallelism to the poetry. Repetition, special vocabulary, and poetic imagery appear in abundance in order to communicate a message. How the poem means may be one of the crucial paths to what the poem means. The language is complex and carries much freight. So attending to the parallel structures and the poetic imagery and the sequencing of poetic language is another important task for faithful interpreters of the Psalms.

A recent volume on this poetry makes a significant contribution to our work. Bill Brown's *Seeing the Psalms: A Theology of Metaphor* explores the poetic imagery of the Psalter in dialogue with the emphasis on the shape of the book of Psalms as a whole.[54] The image of the tree rooted and grounded and growing and producing fruit in Ps 1 as the image of the righteous person is a rich opening image in the introductory poem to the Psalter. The tree appears in the Psalms in various other places, and the meaning is tied to the placement in the book. Brown traces the movement of the tree image.[55] The other image in that introductory psalm is the way or path. The righteous and the wicked follow different paths; the righteous are instructed by the guide of torah and led to life imaged as a verdant tree. The literary settings of these images provide interpretive clues for the careful reader. YHWH as refuge is one of the other metaphors that persists in the poetry of the Psalter. Psalm 2:12 pronounces a blessing on those who seek refuge in YHWH. The lament psalms seek refuge in God: "O LORD my God, in you I take refuge; save me from all my pursuers, and deliver me" (Ps 7:1). Psalm 61 seeks God's help as rock and refuge and the hope for protection under the wings of the divine. This psalm also images the sanctuary itself as a means of divine refuge. Refuge is one of the foundational metaphors of the poetry of the Psalms. Water imagery is also one of the most evocative images in the poetry of the Psalms. The powerful image opening Ps 42 shows that water can quench thirst and bring sustenance. The roaring chaos of water can also bring quick destruction. The poetic language is rich and complex, and it is adaptable for life. The poetry makes it possible for these texts to interface with the lives we lead. "Through metaphor, the psalms paint a world of possible impossibility wherein conflict is resolved and shalom reigns, a world in which deliverance is experienced and sustenance is gained," leading to the uninhibited praise of God.[56] The language is imaginative and portrays God and life in relation with God as part of the community of faith in God's wild creation.

READING TODAY

So I have suggested that reading the Psalms today needs to include the concerns of more traditional modern Psalms scholarship in matters of genre and connections to worship. I have also suggested that where a psalm fits in the sequence of the book of Psalms as a whole is an important question, as is the question about the purpose of the poetic language in these texts. All of these questions come together in what we bring to reading the Psalms. If the Psalms are going to transform us, we must read always in conversation with our life together. Imagine spending time exploring and going deeper with the poetic imagery of the familiar Ps 23 with God as shepherd with rod and staff and the valley of the shadow of death (or however we are to translate the image), and then the table and the cup with God as host at the end of this trust psalm. The last time I preached in chapel at George W. Truett Theological Seminary at Baylor University, I preached on Ps 23, and I don't know how many people said to me that they had often used the psalm but never preached on it or even heard a sermon on it. There is great depth for the faithful there, much for teaching and preaching. Or what about the imagery in Ps 130—the depths, divine forgiveness, waiting for the Lord? The imaginative poetic language provides many opportunities for teaching and preaching and many connections with the lives of readers and communities. The opportunities for growth in faith are remarkable.[57]

One way of thinking about the possibilities is that the Psalter crafts a vision of life as created and sustained by God, not the life peddled by our militant consumerist society but life in which the Lord reigns. And the proclamation of the gospel in Christian worship calls us to embrace that vision as the true vision of life and to live as if it is so. And it will be. The imaginative poetry of the Psalms makes possible such a perception. It is the real truth about life. That is a life-giving grammar of faith.

Psalm 6

Let me illustrate such a grammar and such a reading. Following the introductory Pss 1 and 2, the Psalter launches full force into the world of individual lament with the persistent pressure of enemies in Pss 3–7, which continues in Pss 9–14. Psalm 6 is one of the powerful prayers for help in this opening movement of the Psalter. The text follows the standard structure of an individual lament, opening with an address to YHWH, and then alternates between petition and lament in the first seven verses. The plea is for deliverance in the face of death.

> YHWH, do not punish me in your anger
> or chasten me in your wrath.
> Be gracious to me, YHWH, for I am languishing;
> heal me, YHWH for my bones are troubled (terrified?).
> And I am greatly dismayed
> but you, YHWH—how long?
> Turn, YHWH, deliver me;
> save me for the sake of your unchanging (persistent?) love.
> For there is no remembrance of you in death;
> in Sheol who will give praise to you?
> I am weary with my sighing;
> every night I drench my bed with tears;
> I flood my couch with my weeping.
> My eye wastes away from grief;
> it grows weak because of all my foes. (vv. 1-7, my translation)

One of the interesting things about these first verses of the psalm is that the enemies do not appear until the conclusion of v. 7, though they are still in view at the conclusion of the psalm. The last three verses provide a clear expression of the certainty that God hears the prayer, and the psalm ends with the decisive overthrow of the enemies.

> Depart from me, all (you) evildoers,
> for YHWH has heard the sound of my weeping.
> YHWH has heard my supplication;
> YHWH has accepted my prayer.
> All my enemies will be ashamed and greatly dismayed;
> they will turn back; they will be shamed in a moment. (My translation)

It is not clear who the enemies are, though they seem to function in ways that make the current crisis worse. The verbs in this concluding section of the psalm suggest faith that God has heard the petition and will bring salvation and the overthrow of these opponents.

It is difficult, because of the open poetic language, to be very specific, but it is often suggested that Ps 6 is a prayer of one who is sick and that the prayer was initially part of a ritual seeking healing.[58] The language of vv. 3 and 6-8 suggests that the crisis might be one of sickness, surely a common trouble in faith communities both ancient and modern. At the same time, the poetic language is such that the prayer is not limited to that kind of ancient setting. Worshipers facing a variety of life-threatening crises could pray this lament, just as the prophet Jeremiah lamented about the extraordinary difficulties of his prophetic vocation and made use of the imagery of sickness to do so: "Many persons in communities of faith through the centuries have faced tremendous crises and stood between promise and fulfillment as they prayed Psalm 6."[59]

The imagery of the psalm makes possible an intense plea for YHWH to deliver the lamenter. The very survival of the speaker and the reputation of God are at stake. Quite striking is the reference to the petitioner's bones being terrified in the midst of this languishing near death's door (v. 2). The hallmark plea of the lament psalm comes in v. 3 with the question "YHWH—how long?" The plea is that the One who comes to deliver not delay any longer, for drastic consequences are at hand. Death brings silence from this worshiper and the inability to worship in the sanctuary that brings both refuge and the wholeness the divine presence affords. Sheol marks the experience of being gripped and controlled by the devastating power of death. Verses 6-7 mine the imagery of tears to heighten the sense of crisis at hand. Tears in the night become so abundant that the bed is fully drenched. Grief brings the fading of the eye, the symbol of life. At the end of v. 7, the enemies first appear in the text as part of the trouble and woe at hand.

It is YHWH alone who can bring salvation; YHWH is both the problem and the solution.[60] The divine name occurs several times in the psalm and three times in vv. 8-9 to emphasize the divine response. Repetition marks the correlation between the psalm's petition and response. The lamenter is dismayed in v. 3, and the enemies, whose presence increases in the latter part of the psalm, are dismayed in v. 10. The weeping in v. 6 is answered in v. 8. The verb for hearing is used in vv. 8 and 9 to indicate that YHWH hears and grants the petition; that use of the term is common in the lament psalms. It is also important to note the use of *hesed*, the persistent divine love in v. 4; the petitioner pleads for a sign that God's gracious activity is still at hand. The language of the psalm calls upon readers/hearers to encounter the power of the crisis at hand and the impact of the hope the certainty of divine hearing brings. The clear language of assurance in vv. 8-10 brings the psalm to a positive end. The psalm fervently pleads for YHWH to delay no longer but to come and deliver this one who is in severe trouble. The alternative is death for the lamenter. God hears. The plot of Ps 6 characterizes many of the individual lament psalms.

Believers have prayed Ps 6 through the years in the face of the fear of death—whether because of severe illness or some other extremely disorienting crisis. The grammar of faith articulated in the psalm includes all the experiences of life, even those threatening death, and the words and their poetic use articulate the threat in gripping ways. The faith articulated here is above all transparent, and it is transparent not only in the privacy of the prayer closet but also in the public arena of worship. This cultic prayer fits squarely into the realities of life and death. It is also important that the opponents of life are an integral part of this plea for help in the midst of the ritual. Enemies persist in life and faith. Psalm 6 bears eloquent poetic witness to a brutally honest I–Thou relationship between the lamenter and the One addressed. The persuasive prayer holds the divine One accountable to the teaching of divine hesed, love that persists in the face of dire circumstances (v. 4).[61] A linchpin of the grammar of faith in the lament psalms is candor, both the public claiming of pain and public candor about the power of enemies. This kind of candor is foreign to the culture of prayer in most contemporary settings, but it is put in bold terms in the lament psalms. Essential to the grammar of Ps 6 is that this crisis in life is addressed to the One who can bring full life, the One who comes to deliver. The faith is transparent, and it comes to a clear and powerful hope. YHWH is the One who hears and accepts (vv. 8-9). The emphatic conclusion to the psalm bears witness that YHWH is the God who comes to deliver. The psalm crafts a hard-won grammar of faith in the covenant God in the midst of all life can muster, a remarkable grammar contemporary readers and hearers can appropriate.[62]

Psalm 8

Psalm 8 provides a different example. The text is a familiar hymn of praise to the creator. It is the first psalm of praise readers of the Hebrew Psalter encounter, and it is surrounded by individual lament psalms. The conclusion of the prayer in Ps 7 speaks of singing praises to the name of YHWH, and Ps 8 does just that. It maintains a connection with the surrounding laments by characterizing the creator addressed in those prayers for help. The psalm begins and ends with the familiar exclamation of praise: "O LORD, our Sovereign, how majestic is your name in all the earth!" It is a classic example of an envelope structure typical of Hebrew poetry, setting off the psalm. So this hymn begins and ends with the same line; in this case the beginning and ending suddenly exclaim praise. It is interesting that the psalm speaks in the first person and addresses God consistently in the second person; the body of the text praises God as creator. The psalm's opening line praises the divine name. In the ancient world, a name was more than an identifier. It spoke of the person's character and here that character is glorious throughout all of creation. The acclamation of praise has royal implications, reminding readers that the Psalms celebrate God's kingship, this God who is praised even in the heavens.[63]

Verse 2 confesses, in line with the lament psalms surrounding this text, that God's reign is opposed by enemies and avengers but asserts itself even in the guise of weakness turned into strength. A citadel is made for the creator, as was the custom in the creation stories of the ancient Near East.[64] The true praise is that the living God creates and sustains and reigns in this world, even with chaos knocking at the door.

> You have set your glory above the heavens.
> Out of the mouths of babes and infants
> you have founded a bulwark because of your foes,
> to silence the enemy and the avenger. (vv. 1b-2)

With v. 3, people begin to see the work of the creator—the work of God's fingers (v. 3)—in the night sky and with its vastness begin to wonder how it is that the creator of such a vast universe bothers with such a small speck as a human being.

> When I look at your heavens, the work of your fingers,
> the moon and the stars that you have established;
> what are human beings that you are mindful of them,
> mortals that you care for them?
> Yet you have made them a little lower than God,
> and crowned them with glory and honor.
> You have given them dominion over the works of your hands;
> you have put all things under their feet,
> all sheep and oxen,
> and also the beasts of the field,
> the birds of the air, and the fish of the sea,
> whatever passes along the paths of the seas. (vv. 3-8)

The two parallel terms for people in v. 4, *'ĕnôš* and *ben-'ādām*, speak of human frailty and connection to the ground. And yet the creator of all has crowned humans with glory and honor, with the *imago dei*, the image of God, tied to human dominion over the earth, that is, responsibility to care for the earth as ancient rulers did for their kingdoms.[65] The clear tie is back to Gen 1 and the creation of humans in the image of God. The poem then rehearses the elements of the creation for which humans are responsible, and comes to a sudden stop—as if the poet is overcome—and recounts the acclamation of praise with which the psalm began: "O LORD, our Sovereign, how majestic is your name in all the earth!"

There is more to the grammar of this enthusiastic worship celebration of the divine sovereign's incredible care for us humans. The poetic structure is central to the psalm's import. It begins and ends with exclamations of the majesty of the living God. In between those exclamations are embraced "all" of creation; the short Hebrew word for "all" (*kol*) makes the point. The very middle line of the poem pauses in v. 4 to single out the place of humans as the focus: How is it that the creator of all should note the human creature, pay heed to such a creature? It is a pondering of amazement and wonder. The psalm's poetic structure brims with theological significance. The psalm begins and ends with God, with humans in the middle, all intertwined with creation. Theology begins and moves to anthropology and ecology. Human dominion is a gift of God. The praise of God is actually the right beginning point to deal with the environmental crisis in which we find ourselves today. The praise and acknowledgment of the creator makes clear that we are not called to the exploitation our science and technology might make possible but rather to care for God's creation. Psalm 8 overflows with wonder and awe at the joy and task of women and men and at the God who creates them and blesses them and cares for them. Yes, these humans suffer, as the neighboring psalms all proclaim, but still live with honor and glory in place and vocation in God's good creation.[66] I find that a pretty remarkable piece of this grammar of faith.

CONCLUSION

This introductory chapter has suggested paths for reading and embracing the grammar of faith that is the Psalter. The concerns of genre, setting, literary context, and poetic form are all formative for generative efforts to interpret and live the Psalms. I have suggested that the Psalter's grammar of faith focuses on prayer and praise. The next two chapters take up those two components of the grammar. We begin with prayer.

2

OUT OF THE DEPTHS

The Psalms Speak for Us Today

PRAYER IN THE GRAMMAR OF FAITH

Aubrey Johnson characterized the individual lament psalms as the backbone of the Psalter.[1] That reality suggests that these psalms provide a major plank in the Psalter's grammar of faith. The form-critical approach to the Psalms has embraced that perspective. The third significant Psalms scholar, in addition to Hermann Gunkel and Sigmund Mowinckel, in the form-critical tradition is Claus Westermann.[2] His work on the Psalms began when he was a prisoner in World War II and profoundly influenced his life of faith and continues to influence scholarship. Westermann claims that at the end of the proverbial day there are two kinds of psalms—plea and praise. The life of faith and prayer, the spirituality of the Psalter, he suggests, moves between these two poles of plea and praise and moves in the direction from plea to praise. It is appropriate to begin with the pleas because they come from the very depths of human experience, where many of us find ourselves and begin to cry out to God. I have titled this chapter with the beginning of Ps 130: "Out of the Depths: The Psalms Speak for Us Today." That is the title of what was one of the popular twentieth-century introductions to the Psalms, by Bernhard W. Anderson.[3] Note the preposition. Certainly the Psalms speak *to* us, but Anderson talks about how they also speak *for* us, pray for us when we do not know how ourselves. To put it another way, the writers of the initial *Interpreter's Bible* said that in these psalms we hear the saints of old pray, and we can stand on their shoulders and pray as they prayed.[4] Molly T. Marshall, under the heading of "The Psalter as Teacher of Prayer," reminds us that this perspective on the Psalms takes us back to the early church and the importance of the Psalms in the prayer life of early theologians, as we saw in the opening chapter.[5] Such praying of the psalms requires readers/hearers to be steeped in this language of human address to God over a long period of time, and in that process the remarkable authenticity and contemporaneity of the Psalms are revealed. These perspectives are in line with what we saw of the Psalms in the previous chapter. Central to the grammar of faith revealed in the Hebrew Psalter, the lament psalms articulate in gripping ways the language of trouble and woe. As congregations and believers read, sing, and pray these psalms, we also learn how to pray.

A SCHOOL OF PRAYER

The book of Psalms begins with an introductory poem that, as is often the case with literary works, gathers the participants in the coming narrative—here, the righteous who pray in the psalms, the enemies who oppose them, and the living God who is addressed in these prayers. The psalm begins with a beatitude affirming the fruitfulness of a lifestyle for the person who does not fiddle-faddle around with the wicked—a paraphrase—but who takes direction from the torah of YHWH and delights in it. Torah is often translated "law," but better renderings are "instruction, guidance, teaching, will."[6] The term comes from a root meaning to shoot. In the ancient world, one gave directions by shooting an arrow in the right direction. In the same way, YHWH's torah directs faithful living. This opening to the Psalter suggests that what follows in the book is also part of God's torah or direction or instruction for living, and I suggest that it is especially direction in one of the central dimensions of that life, prayer. So I take this opening of the book to affirm that, central to its grammar of faith, the Psalter is a school of prayer. With this introductory psalm, the words of the psalms as human prayers addressed to God have also become God's word addressed to humans.[7] This view harks back to the perspectives of the theologians in the early church and Reformation, as we noted in chapter 1.[8] In the Psalter we learn how to pray, even when we are so low that it seems impossible. The Psalms can become the Spirit that articulates our moans. And so we turn specifically to the prayers for help—or laments—in the Psalter. There are more individual laments in the book of Psalms than any other psalm type; they have been appropriately labeled "the backbone of the Psalter."

The Shape of Laments

The lament psalms have a fairly typical structure. They begin with an address to YHWH. These prayers are not simply a cry out, but a cry *to*, a cry to the One who hears and can transform crisis into hope. Quickly the prayer turns to the crisis at hand and portrays it in a variety of ways— putting the trouble and woe powerfully before the covenant God who comes to deliver. Psalm 13 is a parade example of such a prayer. Note how the text characterizes the crisis with questions and with repetition in the poetry:

> How long, O LORD? Will you forget me forever?
> How long will you hide your face from me?
> How long must I bear pain in my soul,
> and have sorrow in my heart all day long?
> How long shall my enemy be exalted over me? (vv. 1-2)

From the dramatic portrayal of the crisis, the prayer moves to petition, to seek divine help. The petitions often carry with them strong motivations, reasons why God should answer the prayer; in this psalm the reasons are the prospects of death for the one praying and the prospect of triumph for the wicked.

> Consider and answer me, O LORD my God!
> Give light to my eyes, or I will sleep the sleep of death,
> and my enemies will say, "I have prevailed";
> my foes will rejoice because I am shaken. (vv. 3-4)

After this powerful cry for help and deliverance from death, this persuasive prayer, comes what is called the sudden change of mood to a positive conclusion. Something happens; we are not given the stage directions. The one praying remembers that YHWH is the covenant God who delivers or remembers the salvation history of ancient Israel or the worship leader speaks a word from God—as happens in a variety of texts in the Older Testament in which a prophet or priest offers a word of hope or healing from God—and suddenly the petitioner exclaims in vv. 5-6:

> But I trusted in your steadfast love;
> my heart shall rejoice in your salvation.
> I will sing to the LORD,
> because he has dealt bountifully with me.

The literature of prayer is replete with such sudden changes, and it is especially noteworthy that nearly all of the lament psalms come to a positive conclusion of praise, vow of praise, or an expression of trust or certainty of a hearing.[9]

In most cases, it appears that the crisis itself has not passed, but what has changed is the perspective of the one praying. Now it is clear that the God who comes to deliver, is present to bless, and speaks words of hope is not the God who will abandon the petitioner to the realms of chaos and death. Repetition with variation is important in poetry, and that is true of the poetry of the Psalms. At the same time, this fourfold structure of address, portrayal of crisis, petition, and positive conclusion is pretty typical of the lament psalms.

The Sudden Change of Mood

The move from crisis to hope is one of the more striking features of the laments, and yet we have little information about this dramatic movement. Some interpreters suggest that the expressions of hope are later additions to the text or that the psalm was spoken as a word of thanksgiving after deliverance from the crisis. We have already noted, however, that in most cases, the crisis itself is still present. Others have suggested that the shape of the ritual has a nearly magical effect or that the venting in the psalms brings healing for the petitioner. The most popular explanation for this sudden shift to the expression of certainty that God hears the prayer, however, is the view articulated by Joachim Begrich that a priestly oracle of salvation has been spoken as part of the cultic setting and the expressions of certainty that God hears the prayer are responses to this oracular word from God.[10] The difficulty is that this word of another voice or any indications of the stage directions at this point in the ritual are missing. Begrich points to salvation oracles in Isa 40–55 as models of such oracular utterances that the prophet has borrowed from the cult.

> Thus says the LORD who made you,
> who formed you in the womb and will help you:
> Do not fear, O Jacob my servant,
> Jeshurun whom I have chosen.
> For I will pour water on the thirsty land,
> and streams on the dry ground;
> I will pour my spirit upon your descendants,
> and my blessing on your offspring.
> They shall spring up like a green tamarisk,
> like willows by flowing streams.
> This one will say, "I am the LORD's,"
> another will be called by the name of Jacob,
> yet another will write on the hand, "The LORD's,"
> and adopt the name of Israel. (Isa 44:2-5)

Caution is in order on the issue because the individual laments do not include any such oracles to confirm a connection between oracles of salvation and the move to hope in these laments. Begrich's view is not without textual basis, however. Texts suggest that divine oracles were part of ancient Near Eastern cultic practice. In the Hebrew Bible, the prayer of Hannah comes to mind. Eli speaks a word of hope to her in response to her lament, and she gives thanks to YHWH (1 Sam 1–2). The Psalms also include direct divine speech. Psalms 50; 81; 82; 95 contain oracles. These oracles, however, take a decidedly prophetic tone, calling the community to faithfulness. Perhaps the most promising of the Psalms texts is Ps 12, a community lament.

> "Because the poor are despoiled, because the needy groan,
> I will now rise up," says the LORD;
> "I will place them in the safety for which they long." (v. 5)

The oracle speaks a divine word of hope to those oppressed by a violent and deceptive society. Such divine oracles are rare in the laments. This example comes from a community lament. My form-critical account of the lament psalms has included both individual and community laments. The structures are similar, but there is more variety among the community prayers and some interpreters would divide the categories more strongly. Divine oracles do not appear in the individual lament psalms. So while this account for the change from trouble to hope in the laments is intriguing, it is not fully established. Indeed, some recent interpreters have suggested that form critics have not read the laments carefully enough. They suggest that the sudden change of mood is neither "sudden" nor consistent. The conclusions of the lament psalms may be more varied than we have traditionally thought. We will return to this topic in chapter 5.

THE QUESTION OF SETTING

The connection between these prayers and worship is clear from the language of the texts themselves. There are many references to the congregation and the sanctuary as well as singing and other acts of worship. The lament psalms especially undercut private and simplistic forms of piety. These most personal of biblical prayers clearly are public prayers. I often think we mistakenly equate the personal with the private. These personally and communally powerful prayers are part of the community's vibrant worship. Such ancient settings for these prayers are indicated in the psalms themselves and also in other texts. First Kings 8 is Solomon's prayer of dedication of the Jerusalem temple. It specifies that prayers for help are to be offered there. We know that the community kept festival and lamented in the ruins of the temple after the Babylonians left it in rubble. Erhard Gerstenberger has also suggested that many of these laments were used in settings of the extended family, with petitions offered in the presence of a priest who had come to visit the sick.[11] Such use moved toward the synagogal community. The particular crises that gave rise to the laments are not easy to determine with a given psalm because the poetic language is sufficiently open to make the psalms adaptable for life. These prayers can be used in various crises in various times, including today, because of this open poetic language. Some of the crises would have included illness; false accusation, such as the kind of gossipy backbiting often heard about in churches; legal accusations; social oppression; or persecution. There are both individual and community laments, crises of persons and of the community such as war or famine. In the midst of such trouble and woe, ancient Israel did what its name implies: it addressed God and struggled with God. It is clear that this community and the persons in it never move beyond the possibility of addressing the living God.

I have characterized the laments as the backbone of the Psalter because there are so many of them. It is important that the first half of the Psalter is dominated by laments from individuals. The second half of the Psalter is dominated by psalms of praise, from the community. That is part of Westermann's move from plea to praise.[12] These two moves—from plea to praise and from individual to community—are closely related and form part of the context in which we preach and teach the Psalms. I think it important that Books I and II are dominated by individual laments, psalms from the Davidic hymnbook, and that with the third book, there is a move to the community and particularly a concern with the devastating crisis brought about by the fall of Jerusalem and the destruction of the temple in the sixth century BCE. The transition that begins with the Psalms of Asaph in Ps 73, centering on profound questions about the justice of life, is important for the shape of the book of Psalms as a whole and provides me with a segue to talk about some additional lament psalms. You may well have already noticed that I am following the route from chapter 1 of looking at the types of psalms and their background in worship and their setting in the Hebrew Psalter as a whole. In these additional examples of psalms, I will also focus on the moving use of poetic language.

Urgent Pleas for Help

Psalms 74 and 79 are prayers in the face of the destruction of the Jerusalem temple by the Babylonians in the sixth century BCE. That destructive experience ended life as ancient Israel had known it. With the death of the temple came the death of any hope for justice, the responsibility of the Davidic king, and any hope for atonement, the purview of the Jerusalem temple priests. The center of their world did not hold. Psalm 74 begins with the same question we saw in Ps 13: "O God, why do you cast us off forever (or completely)?" The question "How long?" comes again in v. 10. Beginning with v. 4, the psalm vividly remembers, for God's ears, the enemy's entering the sacred place and hacking away at the beautiful and ornate temple of Solomon and setting it on fire and bringing it to the ground and desecrating it with their violent presence, desecrating this place of special divine presence. The call is for God to "direct your steps" (v. 3) to the ruins of the sanctuary and remember the destruction.

> Your foes have roared within your holy place;
> they set up their emblems there.
> At the upper entrance they hacked
> the wooden trellis with axes.
> And then, with hatchets and hammers,
> they smashed all its carved work.
> They set your sanctuary on fire;
> they desecrated the dwelling place of your name,
> bringing it to the ground. (vv. 4-7)

The psalm's plea in this profound crisis is for YHWH,[13] still confessed as creator and sustainer in vv. 12-17, to take notice and remember and act as the covenant God who comes to deliver and make possible again life for this community of faith.

> Have regard for your covenant,
> for the dark places of the land are full of the haunts of violence.
> Do not let the downtrodden be put to shame;
> let the poor and needy praise your name.
> Rise up, O God, plead your cause;
> remember how the impious scoff at you all day long. (vv. 20-22)

This complaint and petition continue from Ps 73 to narrate an urgent crisis, here in Ps 74 the obliteration of the Zion sanctuary. The importance of the sanctuary in the resolution of the individual's crisis of theodicy in the previous psalm makes the destruction of the temple all the more disturbing.[14] Psalms 74 and 79 reflect the turn in Book III to the implications of the fall of Jerusalem to Babylon. The plea in Ps 74 is for God to remember "your dove," "your poor" (v. 19) just as God remembered Noah and the animals in the ark (Gen 8:1). The psalm demonstrates that the theological underpinning of the laments is found in covenant theology. The poem is an extended plea for divine action in line with expectations of the covenant God. The crisis is dire, but vv. 12-17 also make it clear that Zion is lost, but God is not.

> The psalm persistently and candidly addresses this God, so the loss narrated is grievous indeed but not final, because God can still be addressed, even from the grip of the powers of chaos. The psalm is a persuasive and honest address to God as a model of prayer in worship. In this public claim of pain, ancient Israel seeks to encounter the only truly life-giving one in all of creation.[15]

The companion piece Ps 79 is equally vivid in its poetic memory, a common poetic strategy in the community laments. The scene is a violent one characterized by gruesome death.

> O God, the nations have come into your inheritance;
> they have defiled your holy temple;
> they have laid Jerusalem in ruins. . . .
> We have become a taunt to our neighbors,
> mocked and derided by those around us.
> How long, O Lord? Will you be angry forever? (vv. 1, 4-5)

The familiar question of "How long?" presses YHWH to remember the congregation and take notice of their severe need, not to remember their wayward past but to notice the heinous crimes of the enemies. The petitions vary but seek divine help and use various poetic images in service of that purpose.

> Help us, O God of our salvation,
> for the glory of your (divine) name;
> deliver us, and forgive our sins,
> for your name's sake. . . .
> Let the groan of the prisoners come before you;
> according to your great power preserve those doomed to die. (vv. 9, 11)

The final verse of the psalm brings some resolution to the prayer, but not without a venomous cry for vengeance on the enemies in the preceding verse. (We will return to the issue of vengeance.) The place of the divine presence, the center of the world for this community, is no more. The Babylonian armies have enacted a harsh history; the pain vibrates through these two psalms. The poetic imagery is incendiary. The rhetoric demands action from the covenant God. These remarkable models for prayer reflect a specific history but in powerfully transparent ways raise the question voiced by worshipers in a myriad of crises: where is God?

Psalm 44 is the first community lament to appear in the Psalter. It is near the beginning of Book II and follows an individual lament (Pss 42–43). The language of Ps 44 is sufficiently open so that deciding its specific setting in one of ancient Israel's defeats is problematic. It has connection with Pss 74 and 79 and could relate to the fall of Jerusalem to the Babylonians in the sixth century, but that is not clear. The theological setting, however, in ancient Israel's covenant relationship with YHWH is abundantly clear. The psalm begins with a recounting of the exodus faith in the God who hears the laments of the oppressed community and comes to deliver. The "Yet" beginning v. 9 is important. Now the community has been defeated and broken, "like sheep for slaughter" (v. 11) and made "a laughingstock among the peoples" (v. 14). The key section begins with v. 17.

All this has come upon us,
   yet we have not forgotten you,
   or been false to your covenant.
Our heart has not turned back,
   nor have our steps departed from your way,
   yet you have broken us in the haunt of jackals,
   and covered us with deep darkness. (vv. 17-19)

The language suggests that the covenant is the Sinaitic covenant, and the allusion to the first commandment in v. 20 confirms that identification. The worshiping community says to God, "Because of you we are being killed all day long" (v. 22). The psalm's conclusion calls for YHWH to arise and "redeem us for the sake of your steadfast love."

"The problem in Ps 44 appears at first to be a problem of covenant theology."[16] The lament is a straightforward protest that YHWH has not kept covenant with ancient Israel, and the prayer insists that YHWH do so! It is a remarkably clear example of the other side of the covenant dialogue; now YHWH is held to account. "Although Israel is regularly capable of lament over loss, here the poetry goes beyond lament to a strident accusation against YHWH for having failed Israel and having carelessly handed it over to its enemies in a shameless military humiliation."[17] God has not remembered the covenant. God acted in ancient Israel's salvation history. The community learned that such events communicate that the covenant God is the One who hears and comes and delivers (Exod 3:7-9). The community here looks for the continuation of the mighty acts of the covenant-making God. Readers of the Older Testament will remember a variety of texts in which ancient Israel is found wanting in covenant obedience, but here it is YHWH who has defaulted. "The final imperative suggests that YHWH can reenter a renewed covenant with Israel by performing covenantal obligations to Israel. Israel has the capacity to hold its partner to those obligations."[18] If YHWH is indeed the sovereign covenant Lord, then God is responsible for what has happened to Israel here.

This psalm's covenant theology is not unlike David Blumenthal's theology of protest in the face of the Holocaust, that God has abused the Jewish people. "As God is angry with us in covenant, so we are angry with Him in covenant. We experience a true anger, which becomes a true moral claim, rooted in our mutual covenantal debt."[19] "The words of Ps 44 affirm that God invites believers to cry out, ask questions, reflect on our own faithfulness, and call God to account for what is happening in our lives."[20] Psalm 44, like the book of Job, does not resolve the issues here, but the concluding petition still addresses YHWH as the One who can bring wholeness because of the divine ḥesed, the divine persistent love.

> The issue of theodicy arises repeatedly, a particular and sustained expression of Jewish faith; the complaints against God are not brief exercises in whining. Rather, the reality of evil in the world presses the question about the goodness and trustworthiness of God.[21]

Psalm 44 is a community lament. An individual lament that is equally accusing of God is the powerful Ps 88, a psalm well known for its distinction among the individual laments. It is the only lament that offers no word of hope in the end. The psalm appears at the conclusion of Book III of the Psalter just before the royal text that indicates the demise of the Davidic kingdom. The petitioner in Ps 88 begins by addressing YHWH as "God of my salvation," but the psalm ends figuratively and literally in "darkness" (v. 18). The lamenter cries out to God and portrays the crisis in terms of death invading life.

> For my soul is full of troubles,
> and my life draws near to Sheol.
> I am counted among those who go down to the Pit;
> I am like those who have no help,
> like those forsaken among the dead,
> like the slain that lie in the grave,
> like those whom you remember no more,
> for they are cut off from your hand. (vv. 3-5)

And the trouble is God's doing; note the use of the second person in vv. 6-7 ("you," "your wrath," "you," "your waves"), "you" twice in v. 8 and again in the questions in v. 14; "your wrath," "your dread" in v. 16; and "you" again in the final accusation in v. 18. The lamenter accuses God of the oncoming death.

It is often suggested that the prayer comes from one who has been terminally ill since youth (v. 15) and is now completely isolated. John Goldingay has noted the comparison to the experience of those with Alzheimer's disease when life collapses into chaos.[22] Why has God hidden from this petitioner? (v. 14). The lament accuses the covenant God of salvation of defaulting on the divine covenant responsibilities. Alone and in "darkness" is this worshiper; all that is left is the address to God. The lesson of prayer is abject transparency in persistent dialogue. What a stunning grammar of faith that gives pause!

Psalm 60 provides an interesting example of prayer that is set in ancient Israel's history but put in a way that makes it difficult to specify the events recounted in poetic imagery.[23] It is set among a series of laments in Book II. The lament reflects a defeat for this people, portrayed with the image of an earthquake.

> You have caused the land to quake; you have torn it open;
> repair the cracks in it, for it is tottering.
> You have made your people suffer hard things;
> you have given us wine to drink that made us reel. (vv. 2-3)

The imagery is of an earthquake but the second person ("you") makes it painfully clear that the defeat is at the hands of the covenant God. Then, beginning in v. 6, we find direct divine speech, an unusual salvation oracle, which affirms that God is sovereign over all the lands and has chosen Ephraim and Judah. Verse 8 poetically depicts the defeat of the traditional enemies of Moab, Edom, and Philistia. This oracular word is at the structural center of the poem. The text then returns to prayer.

> The prayer as a whole demonstrates the tension within which God and Israel live. It is a bold and faithful relationship where Israel can accuse God of deserting them and God can answer by declaring God's power as Creator and King of all the world, both within and outside of the borders of Israel. The prayer pulls the hearer this way and then that in the endless tug-of-war between God and God's people. It speaks of doubt and hope. It speaks of how Israel is to cry out to God, even when God seems to be absent.[24]

Psalm 126, set among the Songs of Ascents, bases a petition for the community on a previous deliverance recounted in vv. 1-3. Some would associate the past restoration with return from exile, but the language is much broader than a reference to a single event.[25] The petition uses agricultural imagery to address YHWH, first with the image of restoring wadis in the rainy season and then with the imagery of planting and harvesting. The plea is that those who carry the seed and go out to sow will reap and come home shouting with joy (vv. 4-6). The plea is for a bountiful and timely restoration.

> Restore our fortunes, O Lord,
> like the watercourses in the Negeb.
> May those who sow in tears
> reap with shouts of joy.
> Those who go out weeping,
> bearing the seed for sowing,
> shall come home with shouts of joy,
> carrying their sheaves.

The petitions in these lament psalms are rich with imagery related to the life of the community.

Prayers from Individuals

A few more examples from individual laments give me an opportunity to move more deeply into this cheerful language. We saw in the introductory chapter that Ps 6 is likely a prayer from one who is sick. Note again the strong poetic imagery.

> Be gracious to me, O Lord, for I am languishing;
> O Lord, heal me, for my bones are shaking with terror.
> My soul also is struck with terror,
> while you, O Lord—how long? (vv. 2-3)

We often today speak of terrorism but not often of our bones shaking with terror. The very self is terrorized. What a profound portrayal of those who suffer from debilitating cancer! The plea is for the covenant God to remember this faithful one and come to deliver.

> I am weary with my moaning;
> every night I flood my bed with tears;
> I drench my couch with my weeping.
> My eyes waste away because of grief;
> they grow weak because of all my foes. (vv. 6-7)

And then suddenly with v. 8 the change of mood takes place, and God hears the tears of this prayer and the enemies are suddenly terrified.

Psalm 31 provides a nicely representative example of the cries for help in Books I and II of the Psalter. The crisis at hand could be fairly characterized as centering on malicious gossip against the petitioner. The imagery of the introductory plea makes clear the song's mix of cry for help and expression of trust as well as the psalm's use of the stock imagery of individual laments.

> In you, O LORD, I seek refuge;
> do not let me ever be put to shame;
> in your righteousness deliver me.
> Incline your ear to me;
> rescue me speedily.
> Be a rock of refuge for me,
> a strong fortress to save me.
> You are indeed my rock and my fortress;
> for your name's sake lead me and guide me,
> take me out of the net that is hidden for me,
> for you are my refuge.
> Into your hand I commit my spirit;
> you have redeemed me, O LORD, faithful God. (vv. 1-5)

The physical dimensions of the persecution come to light in vv. 9-10, with similar uses of the eye and the bones as in Ps 6 to suggest bodily suffering. The imagery of death and brokenness follows in vv. 11-13. Adversaries are certainly central to the persecution endured and the isolation it brings. The poetic imagery is at pains to emphasize the contrast between the faithful lamenter and the evil enemies with their "lying lips" and "contentious tongues" (vv. 18, 20) in service of their malicious scheming against the petitioner.

A number of commentators note that the sequence of the psalm is not terribly logical. A second petition seems to begin at v. 9. The psalm is a striking mix of plea and expression of trust that fits the trouble that occasions the prayer. It suggests that the honest dialogue in the laments is itself a bold act of faith. "Psalm 31 is a poem recording the ups and downs of a relationship with God."[26] Some have suggested that the psalm is reminiscent of the experience of the prophet Jeremiah, who is a remarkable example of enduring faithfulness and yet one who suffered through severe encounters with opponents who plotted against him and brought forth powerful expressions of lament in the tradition of the Psalms. "Poetry is meant to engage our memories and our imaginations and in that transform our relationship with God, so the meaning of this psalm is to examine the thin line between faith and doubt that we all share as we strive to better understand and embrace our relationship with God."[27] The concluding section of the psalm makes it clear that the lamenter perseveres in faith in the face of the crisis at hand. The psalm concludes with an address to the congregation urging the faithful to take courage and "wait for the Lord" (v. 24). The psalm speaks its strong petition by way of many metaphors characteristic of laments and bases the appeal for help in the persistent divine love (*ḥesed* in vv. 7, 16, 21). The one praying was "beset as a city under siege" (v. 21) and has endured to encounter the persistent divine love in the face of severe threat (v. 13). The lament calls God to enact the covenant promise of accepting the plea of this believer.

Psalm 55, also in Book II, reflects a crisis of persecution described as "fear and trembling" and "horror" (v. 5). Enemies bring "terrors of death" (v. 4) upon the complainant who wishes "to fly away and be at rest" (v. 6). The speech of these enemies is described as fraudulent words that bring violence and strife (vv. 9-11). The persecution violates the covenant community, and this one speaks of it from the perspective of one who is oppressed by evil opponents and especially by one who used to be friend and companion.

> It is not enemies who taunt me—I could bear that;
> it is not adversaries who deal insolently with me—
> I could hide from them.
> But it is you, my equal,
> my companion, my familiar friend,
> with whom I kept pleasant company;
> we walked in the house of God with the throng. (vv. 12-14)

Gerald Sheppard has suggested that, since the opponents in these texts are in most cases also members of the covenant community, the texts would have been overheard by the opponents and thus become warnings to the enemies, warnings about their covenant unfaithfulness.[28]

One of the markers for English readers of these texts is the important conjunction "but" indicating a change that is coming in the prayed poem (vv. 16 and 23 in Ps 55). Readers should note the contrasting implication of the conjunction. The contrast is between faithful lamenter and faithless enemies. The covenant God who hears and comes to deliver will redeem the lamenter from this persecution (vv. 16-19). The companion and compatriot oppressors violated covenant with plots against the petitioner and others faithful to covenant. The covenant promise is that God hears the community that is persecuted and brings hope for the faithful but a harsh comeuppance for those who violate covenant. "This psalm eloquently reflects the emotional roller coaster of one in pain. The twists and turns allow the audience to enter into that emotional territory."[29]

At the psalm's conclusion, the lamenter calls the community to "cast your burden on the LORD" (v. 22). It is to the covenant God who hears that the community is boldly to address their cries for help. Commentators again note the comparison with the difficulties the prophet Jeremiah faced in the faithful living out of his call. Companions and even relatives persecuted him and derided him. "There is something strangely modern in a poem that begins with a depiction of the self shattered by injustice in the form of a corrupt city and false friend and ends with that same self calm and hopeful, having gone through a process of healing... The poem hides nothing from God out of the conviction that one's inner and outer life belong wholly to God."[30] Goldingay titles his treatment of the prayer "How to Throw Things at YHWH."[31] His list of what the psalm encourages people of prayer to include in their address to God, such as specific oppression and turmoil and especially sexual violence done to women, powerfully reflects the poetic language and setting of Ps 55.[32] "The speech of complaint is an exercise in candor in which the speaker describes a situation of alienation and violence" in gripping poetic language.[33]

Psalm 61, also among the laments in Book II, uses familiar language: From the end of the earth I cry to you, O God, when my heart is melting like wax, from the end of life, just on the cusp of falling into the power and realm of death.

> Lead me to the rock
> that is higher than I;
> for you are my refuge,
> a strong tower against the enemy.
> Let me abide in your tent forever,
> find refuge under the shelter of your wings. (vv. 2b-4)

The plea is for refuge or asylum or sanctuary, offered by the protecting God of the sanctuary. The poetic imagery of these prayers continues to find profound currency in today's life and experience. Central to the full appropriation of the Psalms is our genuine interaction with these images. YHWH offers a high rock, a tower of defense, and shelter of wings—powerful sanctuary images. "The whole of the psalm moves from cries of pain and loneliness to wishes and petitions for abundant life and praise."[34]

One additional image to note is the hunting image, here in one of the prayers from the final Davidic collection of psalms, Ps 142:3b-4.

> In the path where I walk
> they have hidden a trap for me.
> Look on my right hand and see—
> there is no one who takes notice of me;
> no refuge remains to me;
> no one cares for me.

The petitioner seeks release from the prison of trouble and woe (v. 7) and so

> I pour out my complaint before him (YHWH);
> I tell my trouble before him. (v. 2)

The brief prayer articulates an honest and poignant plea adaptable for many crises in life, especially those including both isolation and enemies. The life of the worshiper includes the inseparable mix of petition and trust, trouble and assurance, all included in this seemingly simple song. Several commentators note the character of this psalm in terms of a model for prayer.[35]

FALSE ACCUSATIONS

Several of the individual lament psalms in Books I and II use language that seems to reflect some kind of legal setting. Enemies have accused the petitioner of some wrongdoing, and the petitioner brings the accusation to the supreme judge for acquittal. Naboth would be a good Older Testament example of one who is falsely accused. Psalm 26 is a cry for vindication from one who claims integrity or wholeness in the relationship with YHWH. The extension of the introductory plea hints at an oath of self-imprecation in v. 2. The petitioner asks that the divine judge test the claim of integrity.

> Vindicate me, YHWH,
> for I have walked in my integrity,
> and in YHWH I have trusted without wavering.
> Examine me, YHWH, and try me;
> test my inward parts and my heart.
> For your persistent love is before my eyes,
> and I walk in your faithfulness. (vv. 1-3, my translation)

It is important that the motivation for the initial plea is the divine ḥesed we'emet. The claim of integrity is based in the divine persistent love and fidelity. The petitioner continues by professing faithfulness in vv. 4-5. Verses 6-8 suggest a cultic setting with the altar and the practice of singing a confession of what the covenant God has done. The psalm's conclusion also suggests the worship setting. Much of the psalm is akin to a protestation of innocence perhaps of some accusation, though the particular crisis that occasioned the plea is implicit as is often the case in the poetic prayers of the Psalter.

> Take me not away with sinners
> or my life with the blood guilty
> in whose hands is evil device
> and whose right hand is full of bribe.
> But I walk in integrity;
> free me and be gracious to me. (vv. 9-11, my translation)

The petitioner emphasizes the contrast with the enemies. The psalm emphasizes the divine name and the sanctuary as the place of the divine name. There the community's and the believer's faith is nurtured in the divine presence. There is refuge there and the hope of justice. The lamenter there seeks vindication from the covenant God who comes to deliver. Note the verbs of petition: vindicate, examine, try, test, do not take away, free, be gracious.

Psalm 7 petitions with the use of legal language. Following the introductory plea, it moves through an oath of self-imprecation and a call for the covenant God to judge between the accusers and the petitioner. The accusers are like a wild animal that hunts down the prey and tears apart this one who prays. Contemporary readers of this prayer may well stumble over the petitioner's claim of innocence. Two perspectives are important. In the psalms from those who are falsely accused (such as Ps 7), the claim of innocence is not a claim for perfection or a theoretical claim of blamelessness in all of life. The claim of innocence, as reflected in the oath of self-imprecation in Ps 7:3-5, is a claim of innocence in the face of a particular false accusation.

> O Lord my God, if I have done this,
> if there is wrong in my hands,
> if I have repaid my ally with harm
> or plundered my foe without cause,
> then let the enemy pursue and overtake me,
> trample my life to the ground,
> and lay my soul in the dust.

The petitioner has not done the evil pressed in the accusation from enemies. The comparison with the character Job comes to mind. That book begins with the affirmation that Job is a righteous man who seeks God rather than evil. And thus Job seeks an examination by the righteous judge in his extended orations of lament and especially in his summarizing complaint in ch. 31. The second perspective is a theological one. The understanding of righteousness in the Psalms is not about self-righteousness or always doing the right thing. The term has the sense of right relationship. The covenant God initiates a relationship with the covenant partners, and that relationship is to be embodied in human relationships. Thus, the claim of righteousness by the lamenter is a claim of living in that relationship based in divine initiative. "The righteousness and fidelity of God, then, are the true bases of all prayer but especially of any prayer in which a petitioner pleads his or her own innocence."[36] The prayer moves toward the hope of vindication. One way of thinking about the pressing issue in the prayer of Ps 7 is that the petitioner struggles with a disjuncture between the received covenant tradition that God is the righteous judge and will bring justice and the current crisis of trouble because of an unjust accusation. Carleen Mandolfo has shown that the psalm's emphasis on God as righteous judge comes from another voice seeking to teach the petitioner again the Deuteronomic covenant faith based in the righteousness of God.[37]

Psalm 64 also comes from a crisis centering on malicious words used by opponents. The language is not legal in tone and so perhaps malicious gossip would be the best characterization of the problem. The imagery of the language is again of the hunt; the enemies scheme with words against the petitioner. The language of the covenant God's deliverance of the lamenter uses the same imagery.

> But God will shoot them with an arrow;
> suddenly their defeat will come
> and their tongues will cause it to come upon them. (vv. 7-8, my translation)

The power of words permeates the imagery and language of this prayer. The gossipers trust in the power of their words, but in the end the words bring them to dust. They think they are scheming against the lamenter in secret, but they are publicly humiliated. The verdict and sentence, which overwhelm the enemies, correspond remarkably to the evil they have done. The righteous judge enacts covenant justice. The prayer bears eloquent witness to the power of words. Articulated evil continues to be pervasive and powerful in human experience and to bring powerful distress and chaos. "Of remarkable importance is the reality that the final word of the psalm is not one of chaos but of praise and thanksgiving to the living God, who embraces the pain of those who trust."[38]

Readers of these psalms are often uncomfortable with the approach of these petitioners, who speak of their integrity and even righteousness. It is important to understand the language. The petitioners make clear that their faith begins in the covenant God's initiative. What the lamenters claim is faithfulness to their commitment to the covenant relationship with YHWH. Based on that, they very straightforwardly address the covenant God and candidly insist that YHWH fulfill the divine side of the covenant and deliver from the crisis at hand. "The bold language of the complaint, in short, rests on an intensely personal, trusting, and empowering relationship between God and the petitioner."[39]

A MINORITY VOICE

We have noted a number of psalms that could be classified as psalms of innocence. There are also psalms of penitence, but there are far fewer of these and so I dub them a minority voice. This reality about the Psalms will surprise many Christians. Many of us think of prayer primarily in terms of penitence and the search for forgiveness. The Psalms work primarily out of a covenant theology in which ancient Israel and lamenters therein pray as full partners in the covenant relationship with YHWH. The petitioners assert initiative in addressing God with the trouble and woe at hand. At the same time, the tradition of the church has noted the presence of this minority voice of prayers of penitence. There is an ancient tradition of seven psalms of penitence—Pss 6; 32; 38; 51; 102; 130; 143. A number of contemporary commentators doubt that characterization for several of these texts. We have already seen, for example, that Ps 6 is not unlike other laments. It is, no doubt, included in the psalms of penitence because of its reference to divine anger, but the text does not actually contain any expression of penitence.

Psalm 51, on the other hand, is a powerful psalm of penitence.[40] It begins with a remarkable plea for forgiveness.

> Have mercy on me, O God,
> according to your steadfast love;
> according to your abundant mercy
> blot out my transgressions.
> Wash me thoroughly from my iniquity,
> and cleanse me from my sin.
> For I know my transgressions,
> and my sin is ever before me. (vv. 1-3)

The vocabulary of sin and the imagery of washing and cleansing permeate the psalm. The lamenter has suffered the same troubles as the lamenters in other psalms of complaint: the sentence of the divine judge (v. 4), crushed bones (v. 8), and the fear of divine absence (v. 11). What is different is that the cause of the trouble and woe at hand is within the very life of the petitioner; the trouble is self-inflicted and thus the speaker pleads for forgiveness and restoration.

> Create in me a clean heart, O God,
> and put a new and right spirit within me.
> Do not cast me away from your presence,
> and do not take your holy spirit from me.
> Restore to me the joy of your salvation,
> and sustain in me a willing spirit. (vv. 10-12)

Divine forgiveness and restoration will bring thanksgiving from the petitioner, who will teach others of God's ways. The psalm teaches that such a renewed and contrite spirit is the most faithful attitude in offering cultic sacrifices. The language of the psalm is thick with the vocabulary of sin and petitions for forgiveness. Beginning with v. 10, however, the psalm moves toward anticipation of renewal. It is anticipated rather than accomplished, but there is a shift in the second half of the text.

Already in the opening verse, the speaker intones the familiar reality that the resolution to the crisis at hand is found in the persistent divine love (ḥesed). Striking about this psalm are both its transparency and its intensity. The prayer addresses God in penitence and in honesty and characterizes the experience of brokenness by way of transgression and then pleads for help. The second part of the psalm looks toward hope of restoration. The last verses of the psalm make clear that the prayer is tied to the context of worship. So while the portrayal of the crisis at hand is different, the lessons for prayer in this psalm parallel the lessons from the majority voice in other lament psalms. It is a genuine covenant transaction of confession and forgiveness, long honored in Judaism and Christianity (Ps 103:8-9).

Psalm 130, another of the seven penitential psalms, brings the title of this chapter: "Out of the Depths." The plea comes out of the very depths of human experience, the threatening and chaotic depths.

> Out of the depths I cry to you, O LORD.
> LORD, hear my voice!
> Let your ears be attentive
> to the voice of my supplications! (vv. 1-2)

There is a sense of iniquity and the plea for forgiveness, but the petitions are insistent. Forgiveness is the mark of the covenant God. This brief psalm uses vocabulary and repetition and imagery to intensify the prayer. The lamenter "wait(s) for the LORD"

> more than those who watch for the morning,
> more than those who watch for the morning. (v. 6b)

This individual prayer concludes with the lesson for the congregation based on vv. 1-6. Divine forgiveness is based in YHWH's persistent love, and that is what will restore the community from the threatening and chaotic depths brought on by iniquity. The honest and persuasive plea seeks to renew the life-giving covenant relationship between God and ancient Israel.

We have already noted that Book I of the Psalter is dominated by individual lament psalms. Psalm 32 is such a lament, with characteristics of both penitence and instruction. The lamenter suffers under the strain of self-inflicted transgression.

While I kept silence, my body wasted away
through my groaning all day long.
For day and night your hand was heavy upon me;
my strength was dried up as by the heat of summer.
Then I acknowledged my sin to you,
and I did not hide my iniquity;
I said, "I will confess my transgression to the Lord,"
and you forgave the guilt of my sin. (vv. 3-5)

The lamenter now tells the truth in this prayer and confesses the sin and seeks forgiveness, rather than attempting to conceal the sin from God. The speaker, based on this experience, then teaches God's ways to others:

I will instruct you and teach you the way you should go. (v. 8)

Thus, "the way you should go" (v. 8) points to the psalmist's example of breaking silence to confess sin (vv. 3-5) and to his or her conviction of God's willingness to forgive and restore (vv. 7, 10). The psalmist's witness in vv. 6-11 is in essence an invitation to others, including the readers of Ps 32, to confess their own sinfulness and to live in dependence upon the grace of God.[41] The candid confession of sin to YHWH is at the core of a covenant life of prayer. "Clearly, the ancient Israelites had already understood the truth that 'silence kills' long before Freud reintroduced this Jewish insight into the modern world."[42]

Psalm 38 also powerfully articulates the experience of this silent festering of guilt to the point of "no health in my bones because of my sin" (v. 3).

My wounds grow foul and fester
because of my foolishness;
I am utterly bowed down and prostrate;
all day long I go around mourning. (vv. 5-6)

The ill-health is both physical and social. The clear confession of sin (v. 18) in this transparent prayer is to the One who can respond.

But it is for you, O Lord, that I wait;
It is you, O Lord my God, who will answer. (v. 15)

THE ENEMIES

I should conclude with a few comments about these pesky enemies that keep showing up in the cries for help. It seems that the presence of enemies is persistent, even inevitable in the crises portrayed in these texts. Remember that Westermann suggests that there are three characters in these psalms—the righteous (that is, the petitioners), the enemies, and God. Especially if you read Pss 50–60 in order, you could title them as prayers in the face of enemies and then more enemies and then even more enemies and still more enemies and on it goes. Sometimes in the Psalms the enemies are national enemies, such as in the community laments related to battles, but most of the time the enemies are other people within the community. It is difficult to be very specific about the identity of these opponents of the ones praying and of God. In some texts, the enemies appear to be false accusers, in others oppressors of the faithful, in others those who gloat over the trouble and woe the petitioners are enduring. One of the best biblical analogies is the three "friends" of Job—Eliphaz, Bildad, and Zophar. They have not caused the crisis, but they certainly exacerbate it with their well-intentioned yet dreadful speeches toward Job. At times, I think the enemies in the individual prayers for help in the Psalms are not unlike the kind of backbiting we have all enjoyed in church life, and perhaps even in church staff relationships. I have on occasion characterized these opponents as "frenemies."

The prayers against the enemies are particularly troubling to Christians as we read the Psalms. Take as an example the prayer in Ps 59 that fervently asks for rescue from "my enemies," who are characterized as howling jackals prowling around the city, scavenging by way of their dirty tricks.

> Desperadoes have ganged up on me,
> they're hiding in ambush for me. (v. 3a)
> . . . .
> Bring them down in slow motion,
> take them apart piece by piece.
> Let all that mean-mouthed arrogance
> catch up with them.
> Catch them out and bring them down
> —every muttered curse
> —every barefaced lie.
> Finish them off in fine style!
> Finish them off for good!
> Then all the world will see
> that God rules well in Jacob,
> everywhere that God's in charge. (vv. 11b-13 MSG)

And I have not even gone to the parade examples of imprecatory prayers in Pss 109 and 137, the first a prayer against those who accuse the petitioner and the second the (in)famous psalm that begins with the powerful expression of exile and grief in a foreign land and ends with the chilling beatitude for those who bash the Babylonian babies against the rocks. These painful cries are powerful. Yet Jesus has told us to love our enemies, and indeed such texts as Ps 51 seek for us all a renewed and clean heart. How do we deal with these prayers of imprecation or vengeance? Well, perhaps the first thing to note is that the challenge for the renewal of the heart or for the love of enemies assumes that we have enemies. Any faithful human will find opposition in the world. We need first to admit that reality. Opposition to faithfulness is inevitable.

The Psalms are interested in a process of moving to renewed and cleansed life and suggest that believers must go through these hard feelings in order to get to that point. Honesty and prayer are essential in that process, for these prayers address the One who can actually deal with the issue. Such direct and honest and bluntly intimate prayer language makes it possible to work through such realities of evil and opposition so that it does not fester and cause us considerable spiritual dis-ease. I still remember the question raised in a seminar on the Psalms I led at our church in Waco on these matters. One of the stereotypical grandmothers in the group said, "Can I really pray these prayers because I am having a real problem with someone right now and I need help?" "Molly," I responded, "you had better pray these prayers as part of the spiritual discipline of the honest dialogue of faith so that you can get to a renewed heart and have hope of loving your enemies. Otherwise, you will find yourself mired in the mud of continuing resentment and trouble." Such prayers make the hope of renewal possible. They are not all, but they are part of the movement toward grace in which trust in the One addressed with this part of life also is essential.

Psalm 109 is the strongest of the individual prayers of imprecation. The text begins, "Do not be silent, O God of my praise." It then pleads with YHWH that enemies have mercilessly attacked the petitioner "with words of hate" (v. 3). The petition beginning in v. 6 will curl the hair of even a balding Psalms commentator.

> May his days be few;
> may another seize his position.
> May his children be orphans,
> and his wife a widow.
> May his children wander about and beg;
> may they be driven out of the ruins they inhabit.
> May the creditor seize all that he has;
> may strangers plunder the fruits of his toil.
> May there be no one to do him a kindness,
> nor anyone to pity his orphaned children. (vv. 8-12)

Even this harsh venom comes to an end in v. 19. This petitioner has been harshly falsely accused and is "poor and needy" (v. 22) and completely without resource or recourse. The plea is to YHWH for help, to hear the cry for help in oppression and to come to deliver. Such divine action would be an expression of the divine persistent love (vv. 21, 26). It would be deliverance of the oppressed.

Verses 6-19 are a great embarrassment to Christians; they express the drive of vengeance so present in American society: the punishment should fit the crime. The words are so harsh that the NRSV places a seemingly innocent "They say" at the beginning of v. 6 to suggest that the words are the accusations of the enemy against the petitioner. That is not without basis in the Hebrew grammar, but the addition is without textual basis. The best route is to see these imprecatory words as from the petitioner.[43] The psalm does not in fact support a thirst for vengeance. I actually take it to be a nonviolent text, for it puts the expression of vengeance in prayer addressed to YHWH who claims, "Vengeance is mine." (Deut 32:35). God is the one who can deal with such devastating realities. One could act out vengeance in violence or deny vengeance and suffer the effects of its festering or express the vengeance to God. This psalm takes the latter option.[44]

Psalm 137 is probably the best known of the imprecatory psalms. It "has the distinction of having one of the most beloved opening lines and the most horrifying closing line of any psalm."[45] The psalm begins with the powerful expression of grief at the fall of Jerusalem to the Babylonians. There the community remembers the beautiful songs of Zion and the familiar and comfortable life they had back home. The final three verses lash out in a remarkable set of beatitudes for those who give Babylon and allies their just deserts and the end of their military dominance with the violent deaths of their babies. Contemporary readers are often shocked by the conclusion of the psalm. It is important to remember the particular sociohistorical context out of which the community lament came. The petitioners are powerless exiles; the psalm deals with the harsh realities of war. This song grieves over the loss of the Zion songs and becomes "a bold act of faith as it boldly claims pain and 'takes it to the Lord.'"[46]

These frenemies are one part of the experience portrayed in these cries for help as a sojourn in Sheol, the place or realm of the dead. The petitioners are gripped by the power of death, the dreadful power that has invaded life and diminished it in some way. Imagine the terror of being gripped in the deadly mouth of a lion. In some texts in the Older Testament, Sheol is portrayed as a walled, fortified city one enters and the gate closes behind and the bar goes down and there is no return. The beings there are named Shades, zombies who exist but do not live and do not encounter community or the presence of God. It is a gray, shadowy place akin to the black lagoon swamp with moss and those zombies of old horror-movie fame. What is remarkable about these lament psalms is that these petitioners cry out to YHWH while gripped by the power of Sheol, and they come eventually to a hard-won hope. The psalms portray the surprising, even stunning move from disorientation to new orientation, from death to life, from crucifixion to resurrection. It is essential to see that resurrection only comes through death. We cannot deny pain and death or avoid it but must go through it to get to new life. I find it remarkable that the Psalms make the move from the grip of the power of death to this glimmer of hope. Remember that the paradigmatic lament Ps 13 ends with "I will sing to the LORD, who has been good to me" (my translation).

A COVENANT THEOLOGY OF PRAYER

So what are we to make of these texts? The most striking thing about the schooling in prayer in these texts is the model of the honest dialogue of faith. The prayer here is realistic; they pray of life as it is, not an idealistic life as it is supposed to be. You may remember the older movie *The Disciple*, in which the Robert Duvall character spends the night screaming at God. That fits this model of prayer. It is honest, sometimes brutally so.

In these psalms, ancient Israel is articulating theology, making sense of their experience. The faith tradition of the community is that YHWH is the covenant God who comes to deliver. In these prayers, the community is pleading that they are not being delivered and so cry for God to hear their plea. So I take these prayers to be genuine covenant interactions between the people and their God. Often when we think about covenant in the Older Testament, we think of the call for the people to hear God's demand for faithfulness. In these psalms, we have the other side of the covenant dialogue of faith, the cry for God to hear the prayers of the people and act as the covenant God who hears and comes to deliver. Here ancient Israel in the dark underbelly of the dialogue holds God accountable for the faith and history they have learned.

So I take these psalms to be bold acts of faith in the midst of trouble and woe. Here we learn of individual and public prayer. The world of prayer these texts commend is rather different from the culture in which we find ourselves. We live in a culture that seeks to deny pain and death. The Psalms, in contrast, saw long before there were therapists that the way to hope is through fear; the way to real joy is through depression; the way to loving one's enemies is through hostility. Not around these realities but through them. Denial leads to holding grudges, fear, and festering wounds. That is not faith. Rather, speaking boldly to the One who can act, asking God to embrace pain—that is the vision of faith in these texts. The hallmark cry of these prayers is the probing question "How long?" It is more than venting, a cry out; it is a cry to the One who can transform life. This God is the one who accepts these raw and utterly honest prayers. What defines the people of faith—in line with the name Israel—is speaking to God, struggling with God, no matter what. The community never moves beyond the possibility of addressing this God. So I take these prayers to be bold, liberating, and frightening acts. I take the most difficult part of such honest prayer to be the challenge then to put our hand in God's and trust the God of *ḥesed we'emet* (persistent love and trustworthiness) with what happens.

These texts are theological texts. They are addressed to a named, identifiable "You" in the shared faith tradition. They are not unfocused meditation or self-actualization or flattery of the divine, but genuine pastoral addresses to "You," the creator and redeemer, in the I–Thou relationship. Persons of faith pray to King YHWH. The image that begins Ps 42 envisions the reality; the presence of God is as vital to life for us humans as is water for the thirsting deer. The community learns of this covenant God by way of the shared and rehearsed history. YHWH is the covenant God who creates a new community of justice and faith. In our world, such a story as history is stunning and astonishing. These prayers celebrate and insist on that faith. It is a daring faith in the God of *ḥesed we'emet*, persistent love and trustworthiness. Against all the evidence of society, the laments urge upon us a raw faith of candor in the God who does not leave people of faith alone, but comes to deliver, the God who is "merciful and gracious, slow to anger and abounding in steadfast love and faithfulness" (Ps 86:15). These psalms constitute an anguished insistence that leads to honest, passionate hope that will not relent. God, the "You" herein addressed, risks creating a community of worship, faith, and justice and beckons it to trust. That basic beginning leads to this kind of prayer and living faith. I mentioned in chapter 1 the story of Kathleen Norris recounted in her memoir *The Cloister Walk*. The experience of living with the Psalms made these texts available as a resource when she encountered trouble and woe. She found that this communal use of the Psalms worked against the narcissism of our culture. The Psalms became for her shared prayer, and she began to realize that the theology of niceness we so often espouse and live is at heart dishonest. In a new and transforming way, the Psalms began again to feed her relationship with God and the community. She was again learning to pray by way of these texts, and she saw that their spirituality is theocentric and relational and communal. Such an encounter with the Psalms requires living with them over time and oft-practiced ways. These texts pray in realistic ways and so are amazingly authentic and contemporary, even though they are also ancient.

I think it is difficult for us to get through today's popular piety to experience that transforming reality, and I think it is even more difficult for our congregants to embrace such an experience of prayer. I think some of us will, in our prayer closets, be this honest with God. We can come to realize that the brutally honest language of the lament psalms is the kind of intimate language that characterizes relationships of deep love and connection. These saints of old are intimately in love with God and intimately dependent upon God and saying that in just about as passionate and honest a way as is humanly possible. Luther reminds us of the centrality of the interaction between the stories of our lives and the poetry of the Psalms. The words of the Psalms must somehow become our own words; otherwise, we play a role in a comedy. We use the words in an artificial way.[47] The candid poetry of these psalms can become our own prayers. These texts are unrelentingly realistic about us and about our lives and so call us to pray as we are and as life is. And so the prayers may well reveal the "undertones of our spirits."[48] The language of these psalms may at times seem extreme, but it is language without filters because it is the intimate language of prayer in the covenant relationship with God. Such language at times characterizes prayer. Such powerful and emotional articulation of throbbing pain is a crucial part of the move toward a renewed spirit. But part of what I am calling us to today is that these prayers are also public and relational. Some of us may get to this profound spirituality in our prayer closets, but it becomes even more difficult to embrace in congregational worship. The Costly Loss of Lament is one of the influential articles Walter Brueggemann wrote back in the 1980s.[49] When we do not have lament as part of the worship of the church, we do not model for people growth in their relationship with God. The absence of struggle in that relationship guarantees only stagnation. Further, when we do not have lament in worship, we essentially by way of our dishonest, painless prayers guarantee the status quo. We have no way of calling for God to transform the world, to bring the gospel to reality. How spiritually anemic of us, we of little faith! One of my great fears is that we miss this intimate and troubling language in the prayers of our relationship with God and we never really encounter God at the deepest level. What a loss!

Conclusion

Psalm 22 provides a good summary text for this chapter. It is an individual lament in Book I of the Psalter that illustrates many of the features of lament psalms. It is a general lament characterized by stereotypical language. The lamenter is poor, sick, scorned, near death, falsely accused, and oppressed in a variety of ways. The petitioner brings this overwhelming crisis to God in a lament that makes use of poetry filled with imagery, immediately both adaptable for life and very personal in its appeal. The psalm begins with the standard introductory plea to YHWH and yet does so in a personal way: "My God, my God, why have you forsaken me?" Indeed, the absence of the present God seems to be the crowning issue in this crisis. The pleas in the laments have a generic relationship but are sufficiently varied to be adaptable for life. The initial plea in Ps 22 gives way to a recounting of the basis of covenant theology.

> To you they cried, and were saved;
> in you they trusted, and were not put to shame. (v. 5)

In considerable contrast, the current petitioner lives in shame. The speaker then recounts the personal experience with YHWH as the one who gives life (vv. 9-10). Enemies prowl and death is at hand. The psalm moves through the standard forms of lament in portraying the crisis and pleading for help, especially for the divine presence (vv. 11, 19-21). The sudden change of mood comes at the end of v. 21. God has now heard this plea. The move is striking. Beginning with v. 22, the lamenter gives praise and thanksgiving to God in the congregation. The psalm's concluding verses offer remarkable praise to the sovereign Lord of all, even those yet to come.

The psalm's language is powerful and sophisticated and yet undeniably personal. The first half of the psalm makes it clear that the ancient Israelite congregation is free and unrestrained in professing the abject absence of God. YHWH is nowhere to be found for this one who is praying. That candor is the first and foremost lesson in this school of prayer. That disarming candor is matched by the uninhibited praise of God in the second half of the psalm. Prayer here is enmeshed in the lived experience of faith in a continuous honest conversation. The words of the Psalms can become the words of those praying them in every generation. These psalms teach us of prayer in the grammar of faith.

> In my judgment, until contemporary persons learn to pray the lament as their own, they may not find an avenue to prayer. The threatened existence so many live will find interpretive words to frame their lives in these searing texts. Their grammar of faith will begin to reflect the elusive and mysterious concourse of humans with God.[50]

So amid the power of death, I end with that light of hope, which we will next pursue with the praise of God in the Psalms.

3

THE PRAISE OF GOD IN THE PSALMS

In chapter 1, I suggested that our reading of the Psalms needs to attend to the various types of psalms and their connections with worship as well as the placement of these texts in the context of the Hebrew Psalter along with their poetic language. That language grippingly articulates a grammar of faith for us and our congregations. In chapter 2, I suggested that this grammar of faith persuasively teaches us the art and drama of prayer. I languished in the depths of the lament psalms. In this chapter, I want to come to the praise of God in the Psalms and to suggest that the Psalter also comprises the cantor, or singer, of worship—to borrow a term from Judaism. These texts lead us in worship.

I mentioned Claus Westermann in chapter 2.[1] Westermann claims that at the end of the proverbial day, there are two basic types of psalms: plea and praise. And the life of faith and prayer, the spirituality of the book of Psalms moves between the two poles of plea and praise and moves in the direction from plea to praise. In a sense, here is Westermann's summary of the book of Psalms. The laments plea for God's help and often end with a vow. That vow is fulfilled in the psalms of praise that narrate or declare to the congregation how God has come to deliver. Westermann's narrative or declarative praise is what most of us label as thanksgiving. That kind of praise is related to the psalms of praise that describe God as creator, redeemer, and teacher. So Westermann speaks of two kinds of praise: thanksgiving that narrates divine deliverance from crisis and descriptive praise that broadens the praise of

YHWH in these poetic texts. And so we come now to the vibrant and varied texts that offer praise to God. The texts are full of wonder and awe; Hermann Gunkel speaks of their enthusiasm for God.[2] These psalms sparkle with joy, and they do so with shared literary patterns. Awareness of these can help make us more careful readers of the poetry. I will begin, as I did in chapter 2 with the laments, by looking at the standard structures of praise and then suggest something of the diversity of the psalms of praise with a look at various texts.

The Form-critical Tradition

Declarative Praise

The psalms of praise often begin with a call to praise with verbs in the imperative. The characteristic term is "Hallelujah"—"you all praise Yah," the poetic shortened form of YHWH. You all (y'all) didn't realize that Hebrew was a Southern dialect, did you? It is worth noting that "Hallelujah" is not a word of praise but a call to praise. More grammar! I will return to that point in a bit. Following the introductory call to praise typically comes the body of the psalm that articulates reasons for praise. Some of these texts are lengthy. They may use the relative particle—YHWH *who* creates and redeems and speaks—as the format of the reasons for praise or they may use participles that have the same grammatical effect, or they may use images such as shepherd or host in characterizing God as worthy of praise. Often the poets call upon the short Hebrew word *kî* ("for" or "because") as the key to unlock the reason the community should offer praise to God. Those of us who are academics often spend hours trying to come up with things like that to endear ourselves to our students. A clear illustration of this structure is the shortest of the psalms: Ps 117. The psalm is included in what are labeled as two collections of hymns of praise in Book V. Psalms 111–118 are *hallelujah* psalms, and Pss 113–118 are labeled the "Egyptian Hallel" used during Passover.[3] The text begins with a universal call to praise and then uses the particle *kî* meaning "because" or "for" to articulate the reason for praising YHWH.

> Praise the Lord, all you nations!
> Extol him, all you peoples!
> For great is his steadfast love toward us,
> and the faithfulness of the Lord endures forever.
> Praise the Lord!

And that is the whole psalm. It moves through call to praise, reason for the praise, and renewed call to praise as the conclusion. These psalms often exhibit the poetic envelope structure of beginning and ending in a similar fashion. This basic structure of the body of the psalm predicating the reason for the praise called for in the introduction is central to the praise of God in the Psalms. In articulating the reason for praise, this psalm uses the freighted vocabulary of God's *hesed we'emet*, the persistent divine love and fidelity that does not change with external circumstances. The first term *hesed* was translated *lovingkindness* in the King James Version. I sometimes use *unchanging* or *steadfast love* or *constancy* or *loyal love* or *persistent love*. The second term, *'emet*, indicates fidelity to a promise or trustworthiness or truth; God is worth the trust. You can bet your life on God. This phrase of steadfast love and faithfulness characterizes the God praised in the Psalter. Ancient Israel knows this God by way of the history of God's delivering the community and guiding the community with the divine presence.[4] The persistent love and fidelity of God are powerful, full, and enduring. That calls for celebration. This brief psalm embodies a great deal about the praise of God in the Psalms. It is particularly striking that the call to praise is universal, addressed to "you nations" and "you peoples." The basis for the praise, however, reflects the exodus traditions of ancient Israel ("toward us"). I suppose the first person plural could include all peoples, but the language of *hesed we'emet* seems particularly to refer to the history of ancient Israel. It is likely that the psalm reflects the view that ancient Israel is called to be a means of blessing for all nations (Gen 12:1-3) and not only for themselves. The tension of the universal and the particular runs through the Older Testament. In Ps 117 all people are called to praise because YHWH demonstrates persistent love and fidelity to one people as a means of showing that care for all people. Such a God is greatly to be praised. The structure of call to praise followed by the reason for the praise is central to the praise of God in the Psalms. The dramatic question is how the community will respond to the call for praise.

A particular variation of the theme of this basic structure of praise comes in what I have already described as psalms of thanksgiving. Psalm 30 is the parade example of an individual psalm of thanksgiving. It begins by announcing the purpose of offering praise and thanksgiving and briefly articulates the reason for the praise.[5]

> I will extol you, O LORD, for you have drawn me up,
> and did not let my foes rejoice over me. (v. 1)

The one giving thanks speaks of the experience of deliverance from Sheol, the power of death, restoration "from among those gone down to the Pit" (v. 3). The poetry in the introductory articulation of purpose uses the device of polarities, here of up and down: "I will extol (lift up) you; you have drawn me up." It is also in v. 3 with the bringing up from Sheol and restoration from the Pit. This device powerfully expresses the experience that the speaker cried to God and God healed (v. 2).[6] The use of the language of healing (v. 2) has suggested to many interpreters that the speaker was ill and has been restored. The psalm fulfills a vow of praise and thanksgiving to God as the one who delivers. With v. 4, the speaker turns to the congregation to call them to praise. This psalm is a testimony to God as the one who delivers and invites the congregation to join the narrative and also experience again the power of divine deliverance. The congregation continues to learn and confirm the history of God as the one who delivers.

With v. 6, we come to the body of the psalm and the narration of divine deliverance; the narrative tells the reason for praise. Verses 6-7 portray the crisis. God had given abundance to the speaker, but it came to naught. The crisis leads to the petition in vv. 8-10.

> To you, O LORD, I cried,
> and to the LORD I made supplication. (v. 8)

The persuasive petition leads to the account of the deliverance in striking poetic imagery.

> You have turned my mourning into dancing;
> You have taken off my sackcloth
> and clothed me with joy. (v. 11)

The body of the psalm provides the reason for praise and thanksgiving as a narrative of divine deliverance from the crisis at hand. Life had fallen apart for the speaker, who prayed for divine help and was restored from the sojourn in Sheol, the place of death. The psalm's concluding verse articulates a renewed pledge of praise and thanksgiving.

> So that my soul may praise you and not be silent.
> O LORD my God, I will give thanks to you forever. (v. 12)

Westermann would categorize Ps 30 as narrative or declarative praise. The psalm declares to the congregation the narrative of the crisis and divine help for the one offering thanksgiving. The psalm is a testimony to the confession that YHWH is the God who hears, comes, and delivers.

Narratives of Deliverance. It is important to pause and think about the means of divine deliverance. I suspect that most readers of the Psalms think of deliverance in terms of sudden divine action to bring a person or a community out of a hole; that deliverance would not be possible without divine intervention. That kind of immediate deliverance is present in mighty acts of God in the Hebrew Scriptures. There are also other means of deliverance in the Scriptures. Think of how important the characters Moses, Aaron, and Miriam are in the story of God's deliverance of the people from oppression in Egypt in the account of the exodus. God can deliver by way of humans. There are additional times in the Hebrew Bible in which YHWH makes it possible for people and communities to endure and continue on in the face of trouble and woe; think of Job. That kind of narrative may strain the term "deliverance," but it is clearly one of the ways God helps those in need to find paths forward. The point here is that readers of the Psalms need to take care with their expectations for the means of divine deliverance. If readers expect deliverance to come in only one way (perhaps by a sudden direct rescue), they may be setting up themselves for disappointment. It is the witness of the Older Testament that God delivers in many and diverse ways. That is an important reality to remember in reading the psalms of thanksgiving (and lament). Psalm 30 takes the long view of life, including the experience of trouble and woe as well as deliverance and continuing praise and thanksgiving to God (v. 12).

Poetic Imagery. Before we leave Ps 30, I want to point out the remarkable poetic imagery of how God restores this one who was at death's door. In vv. 4-5 when the speaker turns to address the congregation in the call to enter the experience of thanksgiving for deliverance from crisis, the speaker gives a reason why the congregation should join in with remarkable poetic language.

> For his anger is but for a moment;
> his favor is for a lifetime.
> Weeping may linger for the night,
> but joy comes with the morning. (v. 5)

The psalm's recounting of the speaker's petition in crisis shows again the persuasive language of prayer in the Psalms, and the report of the deliverance—as I have already noted—also employs remarkable imagery.

> You have turned my mourning into dancing;
> you have taken off my sackcloth
> and clothed me with joy. (v. 11)

Lying prostrate with dust upon one, with rent garments and burlap sack as symbolic clothing, communicates great grief. Such has been changed to dancing and new clothing of joy. The intense language of the psalm reminds readers of the strong language of the lament psalms. The articulation of thanksgiving in this psalm demonstrates the community's candor in their praise, a parallel to their candor in lament. A psalm such as Ps 30 suggests a ritual in which the petitioner, now on the other side of a crisis of sickness or oppression or false accusation or famine, has seen divine help and fulfills the vow of praise and thanksgiving to God by telling the story of how God has come to deliver and been present to bless and spoken to guide. Thanks be to the God who brings life out of death; that is one dimension of Israel's worship. The psalm suggests that the goal is not only deliverance but also the transparent praise of God. Robert Alter has noted the "foregrounding of language" here.[7] The power of speech as prayer and praise is important in the psalm as is the divine act of deliverance. These psalms persuasively and candidly lead us in the worship of thanksgiving—telling the story of divine involvement in life.

The community's psalm of thanksgiving begins:

> We give thanks to you, O God;
> we give thanks; your name is near.
> People tell of your wondrous deeds. (Ps 75:1)

This celebration of community worship follows immediately one of the searing laments of Book III, both Psalms of Asaph. The thanksgiving is a kind of response to the community's intense lament, and it is the divine hand who brings thanksgiving to the community. This hope of deliverance leading to thanksgiving is a manifestation of the divine ḥesed (Ps 107) and is tied to the dramatic divine blessing in Pss 124 and 129 in the Psalms of Ascents. Psalm 136 summarizes the salvation history as a liturgy of thanksgiving for the divine ḥesed. Finally, Ps 67 shows that the thanksgiving goes beyond this community so that the peoples are all called to narrate the declarative praise in response to the divine blessing.

These psalms of thanksgiving or declarative praise illustrate the interplay between the individual and the community in the praise of God in this grammar of faith.[8] As noted above, Ps 30 addresses the community with a didactic purpose; Ps 107:33-43 has a similar purpose of teaching the community of the divine ḥesed. Several thanksgiving psalms urge readers and hearers to remember that God is still the God who delivers, and that the lesson is for both individuals and for the community (Pss 34; 66; 92; 136).

The narration of divine deliverance offers declarative praise to YHWH and instructs the worshiping community.

Descriptive Praise

Alongside such testimonies of thanksgiving, Israel's worship also includes the broader adoration and praise of God as creator and redeemer. Such descriptive psalms of praise include a variety of texts. Praise of God as creator and sovereign of all, as well as the God who is present with the community of ancient Israel in Zion, are evident in this praise of God in the Psalter's grammar of faith. These psalms praise God as the trustworthy God who continues to seek fidelity in relationship with the worshiping community. This revelation of the character of the Lord of the Psalms is especially noticeable in the general hymns of praise, often in a recounting of history. The first six verses of Ps 105 call the community to sing praise to God by making known the mighty acts of God among the peoples.

> In form, Psalm 105 may be considered a song of praise, with vv. 1-6 constituting the invitation to praise and vv. 7-45 giving the reasons. In content, Psalm 105 is similar to Psalm 136 in that both psalms focus exclusively on what God has done.[9]

Verse 5 puts it,

> Remember the wonderful works he has done,
> his miracles, and the judgments he uttered.

The verb *zākār*, or "remember," means literally to member again or experience again. I take this call as a singer or cantor of worship, a clue that worship entails rehearsing or recounting or perhaps better, reenacting the mighty acts of God. It is more than sitting and thinking about these things, our passive sense of remembering. It has to do with dramatically living again the salvation history of YHWH for this community. The psalm calls for the congregation to make visible and audible God's awe-inspiring involvement in their history, acts of "abiding astonishment,"[10] divine involvement that makes life possible for the community. The opening verse of the psalm calls the congregation to this kind of praise:

> O give thanks to the LORD, call on his name,
> make known his deeds among the peoples.

The opening imperative *hodû* has more the sense of narrating what God has done than the traditional sense of giving thanks for English readers.[11] So the defining structure of the hymnic praise of God in the Psalms centers on "Hallelujah," or the call to praise, and the reason for praising God; in Ps 105 that reason is the history of divine salvation for the faith community of ancient Israel. This recounting of history that begins in v. 7 constitutes the congregation's rejoicing in YHWH and so praise addressed to God. But the poetry also functions in at least two other directions. It also seeks to persuade the community that God is characterized by *ḥesed we'emet*, persistent love and trustworthiness, and thus God is worthy of praise. Notice that the call to praise also suggests in the very first verse that this recounting of history becomes ancient Israel's witness to other peoples, their telling the story of salvation history to the nations. So the body of this hymn of praise powerfully praises God and instructs ancient Israel and other peoples.

The recounting of history in Ps 105 generally follows the path of the Pentateuch. It begins with the covenant promise to the family of Abram and Sarai, Abraham and Isaac and Jacob and Joseph, and moves to the experience of the exodus from bondage in Egypt with Moses and Aaron and Miriam, the deliverance and the guidance in the wilderness and the journey to the land of promise so that they might craft life as found in the divine instruction. The psalm ends with an echo and renewal of its introductory call to praise, now with the characteristic hymnic term "Hallelujah," Praise the Lord! Such a singing and leading of worship is an indication of the ancient congregation's singing adoration to God as the creator and liberator and shepherd and a clue to us about the character of faith and worship. Here by way of memory, the ancient congregation articulates the life-giving relationship between the living God and the community in their regular worship and in their festal worship.

Psalm 105 appears near the end of Book IV of the Hebrew Psalter. It emphasizes the divine faithfulness to the ancestral covenant promise.

> He is mindful of his covenant forever,
> of the word that he commanded,
> for a thousand generations,
> the covenant that he made with Abraham,
> his sworn promise to Isaac. (vv. 8-9)
> ....
> For he remembered his holy promise,
> and Abraham, his servant. (v. 42)

This persistent fidelity to the ancestral covenant promise brings praise to God, and the congregation again learns the tradition of divine covenant faithfulness. This celebration and reminder of divine persistent love and fidelity is particularly relevant for the community seeking to deal with the aftermath of defeat and exile: "The intent of Pss 105–106 to address the crisis of exile is in keeping with the apparent purpose of Book IV to respond to the theological crisis of exile elaborated in Book III."[12] The juxtaposition of Pss 105 and 106 relates to the needs of the community returning from exile, and it is helpful to read the two psalms together. Psalm 106 recounts the faithless response of the people but in so doing gives focus to divine grace; see vv. 1-3, 43-47:

> For their sake he remembered his covenant,
> and showed compassion according to the abundance of his divine persistent
> love. (v. 45)

Psalm 106 begins and ends with "Hallelujah." The concluding verse of Ps 105 speaks to the purpose of YHWH's salvation history with ancient Israel.

> That they might keep his statutes
> and observe his laws. (v. 45)

The purpose of the divine acts of "abiding astonishment" is that the people might live fully as the community in covenant relationship with YHWH, that is, in line with YHWH's covenant instruction. Praise for God's mighty acts brings glad response in obedience. Such a response hints at the continuation of the covenant promise, an antidote to the crisis of exile. The praise of the ongoing divine commitment to the ancestral covenant promise in Ps 105 as a response to the crisis of exile and its aftermath is also the reason vv. 1-15 of the psalm are recounted in 1 Chr 16, a text that attends to the needs of the downtrodden community still dealing with the implications of exile. The psalm celebrates the divine persistence in covenant fidelity; the covenant promise continues for each generation.

Other Types of Descriptive Praise

I take a step back to Ps 96, a jubilant combination of the call to worship and the reasons for worship. Psalm 96 is part of the important collection of Enthronement Psalms in Book IV. They celebrate the divine kingship in response to the theodical questions raised in Book III with the fall of the Davidic kingdom. The extended and universal call to praise in Ps 96 begins:

> O sing to the Lord a new song;
> sing to the Lord, all the earth. (v. 1)

It may be that this psalm was included in the fall festival complex of the New Year with the celebration of trumpets and the Day of Atonement and the Feast of Tabernacles as delineated in Lev 23. This act of singing a new song to the divine king is the focus of Sigmund Mowinckel's proposal for the liturgy reflected in this and other psalms that celebrate the reign of YHWH: "The impact of the hypothesis is that the liturgy itself is 'effective' in enacting, performing, and dramatizing YHWH's rule."[13] The reign of King YHWH happens "today" in worship. With the New Year comes a new song and a renewal for the congregation of the reign of YHWH and thus a renewed life together. It may well be that Ps 96 itself is the "new song" called for; most of the psalm is used in 1 Chr 16 with the rite of bringing the ark to Jerusalem. McCann suggests, however, that the "new song" could also be a response to a historical moment such as the Babylonian exile, a possibility supported by the use of such poetic language in Isa 40–55. The call could also be in reflection of the not yet, the coming establishment of YHWH's justice and righteousness in the world (v. 13). It may well be that the psalm is pregnant with all three possibilities.[14] Singing a new song is thus a profound act of hope and a call to enact that hope in the realities of life in this world.

Note the call to praise in the first three verses of Ps 96.

> Sing to the LORD; bless his name; tell of salvation from day to day.
> Declare his glory among the nations.

The glory of the Lord is a manifestation of God's presence and activity in the world. The reason for this renewed praise comes in vv. 4-5: The Lord is the creator with strength and majesty and honor and beauty, in contrast to the other gods who are idols (v. 5), empty breaths of hot air who promise the moon and give nothing! The call to praise returns with rising intensity.

> Ascribe to the LORD, O families of the peoples,
> ascribe to the LORD glory and strength.
> Ascribe to the LORD the glory due to his name;
> bring an offering and come into his courts.
> Worship the LORD in holy splendor;
> tremble before him, all the earth.
> Say among the nations, "The LORD is king!" (vv. 7-10)

There is the central affirmation, and James Mays labels it as the central affirmation of the Psalter: the Lord reigns![15] This text is an enthronement psalm, celebrating the kingship of the living God. Verse 10 suggests that the divine rule brings order and justice to life. The call to praise then becomes even more expansive beginning with v. 11.

Let the heavens be glad, and let the earth rejoice;
let the sea roar, and all that fills it;
Let the field exult, and everything in it.
Then shall all the trees of the forest sing for joy
before the LORD; for he is coming,
for he is coming to judge the earth.
He will judge the world with righteousness,
and the peoples with truth. (vv. 11-13)

Remarkable! All of creation is now called to sing a new song of praise to God. Hans-Joachim Kraus, a recent Psalms commentator, has said that is ridiculous; fields don't exult; trees don't sing or the earth rejoice.[16] He has missed the point of the poetic imagery, has he not? The psalm's profession of faith is that any and everything is possible when the Lord comes. And notice again the reason for the praise: "The Lord (YHWH) is coming and coming to bring justice for all of creation." Such is the reign of King YHWH! That confession of faith in the context of praise I find to be stunning in our world. The poetry is poetry of wonder and joy and power.

I am reminded of this passage from Annie Dillard:

On the whole, I do not find Christians, outside of the catacombs, sufficiently sensible of conditions. Does anyone have the foggiest idea what sort of power we so blithely invoke? Or, as I suspect, does no one believe a word of it? The churches are children playing on the floor with their chemistry sets, mixing up a batch of TNT to kill a Sunday morning. It is madness to wear ladies' straw hats and velvet hats to church; we should all be wearing crash helmets. Ushers should issue life preservers and signal flares; they should lash us to our pews. For the sleeping god may wake someday and take offense, or the waking god may draw us out to where we can never return.[17]

This powerful God of persistent love and fidelity is with the worshiping community in the sacred place of Zion where the congregation rehearses and renews its history of faith as in the familiar Pss 46 and 48, coming to the conclusion in the full-throated refrain:

The LORD of hosts is with us;
the God of Jacob is our refuge (Ps 46:7, 11).

"Readers of Book I (Pss 1–41) will recall that YHWH as refuge is one of the significant themes in those psalms. With Ps 46, that theme now surfaces in Book II."[18] The psalm holds three stanzas, the first confessing YHWH as refuge in the midst of chaos, the second and third in the midst of conflict and war. The imagery of the river is important in the second stanza. Since the psalm is about Zion/Jerusalem, interpreters have often wondered about the river, since there is no river in Jerusalem. The imagery is of the sanctuary as the source of water as sustenance for life. The place of the divine presence in worship provides the water necessary to live; see the image at the beginning of Book II (Ps 42). Verse 10 of Ps 46 contains a famous line in the history of meditation in Christian circles: "Be still, and know that I am God." In Ps 46, the line has to do with the divine destruction of war. God, rather than military might, gives abundant life. The psalms of praise again sing the community's worship, our worship, and so lead us to sense the reality of divine engagement with the congregation, an engagement that continues to instruct on worship and its place in the life of faith. Ps 48:9 holds an important word in that instruction.

> We ponder your steadfast love, O God,
> in the midst of your temple.

"Ponder" is a terribly weak translation of the verb *dāmâ*. It has to do with comparison. The best sense is that the congregation represents or enacts and in that way compares; it is important that it is the divine persistent love that is represented or enacted in ancient Israel's worship. So it is appropriate that "Mount Zion be glad" and the community rejoice (v. 11).

The liturgies for entrance into worship in Pss 15 and 24 continue this covenant instruction in the context of the praise of God. The central affirmation is that worship is tied to the rest of life. The preparation for worship espoused in these poems is not of the ritual type but of the ethical type. All of life, inside the sanctuary and outside it, belongs to the creator (Ps 24:1-2). In a prophetic theme, these instructions about entering the sanctuary and the divine presence for worship sing that those with "clean hands and pure hearts" (Ps 24:4) are the ones ready for encountering the divine in worship. The encounter with the divine makes possible full and faithful living, the full sense of righteousness. The Psalms celebrate this God who makes such covenant life possible and continues to instruct the community in the paths that bring life. The *Sitz im Leben* of the praise of God in the Psalms is liturgical where the covenant community sings.

> This identity flows out of an ancient story that continues to take on new life, in words and tunes that speak today. It gives voice to individual people in praise, lament, and need, but it does not leave them isolated, surrounding them instead with a great choir.[19]

Hermeneutical Implications

So what might we say as a worshiping community about this praise of God in the Psalms? First, it is clear that the praise of God is always substantive.

There is always a reason for praising God. The contrast is with contemporary feel-good pep rallies in the guise of worship; those are more akin to the idolatrous rituals the prophets railed against in the ancient world. The praise of God in the Psalms is deep and rich, always substantive.

Second, how does the worshiping community offer praise to God? The Psalms sing the story of how God comes to deliver and is present to bless and speaks to guide. The contrast here is the emotionalism of contemporary mass-media religion where the goal is the momentary emotional high that has little connection to the rest of life and little connection with the history of the biblical faith tradition and little substance. The repeated emotionalistic screaming of the call to worship, "Hallelujah," does not square with the praise of God in the Psalms. You know them, the charismatic-lite choruses of one word, two notes, three hours. My concern is that such emotionalism corrupts genuine faith and leaves many seeing only one alternative in our culture brimming with secularism and its militant consumerism with no place in between for biblical faith. Maybe you have had a similar experience of attempting to relate to people who are puzzled by you because you are profoundly religious, but not in this exhibitionist mode of the religion so often showcased in contemporary media.

Third, the praise of God in the Psalms is honest and unfettered. Here the contrast is with those of us who need to have everything proper. The faith portrayed in the Psalter reveals things done decently and in order but not at the expense of emotion. The praise of God in the Psalms joins emotion and reason. Here it is important to see all of the Psalter and to remember the lament psalms and their bold candor. The candid and powerful articulation of the relationship with YHWH in the psalms of both plea and praise gives the full portrait of true worship. Praise seems hollow without the honest dialogue of faith in the laments, and the loss of lament makes praise into a guarantee that nothing changes so that God becomes serenely irrelevant in heaven, the portrait of Baal against which the prophets railed. That God is foreign to the Psalms—a distant, faintly recognizable deity with kind and gentle words and relationship to only the pleasant parts of life. I fear that the church's worship is part of the problem. It is as if the church does not know how to proceed when faced with an empty secularism on the one hand and empty emotionalism on the other. The Psalms suggest, even insist, that the way of genuine faith is the way of regaining the vibrancy of prayer and praise, the wedding of the intellect and the emotion in the intersection of worship and life with all its joys and deep questions, with a deep trust in the God who comes to deliver, is present to bless, and speaks to guide, the God who engages with this world and life in challenging and troubling ways. The Psalter's schooling in prayer and singing in worship put together a vibrant grammar of faith.

CONTEXT OF THE HEBREW PSALTER

So the praise of God in the Psalms narrates God's involvement with the community in profound and uninhibited chords. I have been insisting that the Hebrew Psalter is a grammar of faith, school of prayer, and singer of worship. The first psalm introduces this massive hymnbook and prayer book by gathering the participants in the songs to follow—God, the righteous, and the wicked. It also raises the most basic decision about living.[20] The psalm begins with a beatitude, and the rendering of its first word is problematic. Most contemporary translators have given up the rendering "Blessed" because that reflects a different Hebrew term indicating a liturgical blessing, not the context in Ps 1. The term here 'ašrê is a wisdom term reflecting a lifestyle. Some have suggested "Happy" as the translation, but it is not what most contemporary readers mean by "happy." It is much more profound and much deeper, perhaps joyful. A recent suggestion is "Contented," but that is too passive. Here, I think, is the point. The 'îš, the person, who is whole, who is put together with integrity, does not fiddle-faddle around with the wicked, does not follow the life advice of the foolish but rather lives fully and faithfully by way of divine instruction, the torah of YHWH. The psalm is built on this contrasting parallel of the righteous or wise and the wicked or foolish. This poem that serves as a kind of preface to the Psalter bathes us in contrasting images of the wise and the foolish. The person who is whole follows not the lifestyle of the wicked but God's direction that is woven into the warp and woof of life. The verbs in v. 1 ("walk," "stand," and "sit" [my translation]) suggest that the psalm is about a lifestyle; God's torah or direction medi-tated on "day and night" guides in that life. The poetic images move in v. 3 to a tree rooted and grounded and nurtured by the waters and so bearing its fruit. Such a grounded poetic image of the righteous is in contrast to the chaff blown away by the wind, the portrayal of the wicked in v. 4. The chaff is the lightweight outer husk of the wheat separated as trash and thus unattached and blown away. Imagine the fluff of dandelions blown willy-nilly by gusts of wind. This chaff has no place to stand when decisions are made in the community. The final summarizing verse of the psalm puts God squarely in the corner of the righteous.

The psalm portrays two lifestyles and encourages the wise, righteous, just, faithful life as the one that bears fruit. I wonder about the righteous and the wicked in our setting. Perhaps we could put the contrast this way. The righteous have oriented themselves toward God and understand life as a divine gift, understand life in terms of relationship with God and other persons. The wicked are self-centered, autonomous, self-sufficient; I would suggest that such a lifestyle leads to alienation and isolation. What the psalm nurtures in us is a portrayal of the faithful person in community and in relationship with God; therein one encounters wholeness or integrity. Such an 'iš is open to instruction and what follows in the Psalter is just that, instruction in the life of prayer. This introductory psalm frames the Psalter as a didactic document.

This poetic conversation, if you will, about life and faith continues as God provides life and leadership to the community, but God's teaching for living is persistently opposed by the pesky enemies, as we see in Pss 2 and 3 and the other psalms to follow. The story with its poetic building blocks moves from plea to praise and from pleas of the individual to praise of the community. The two moves of plea to praise and individual to community are intertwined. The move is to hope in the God encountered in the worshiping community. The book of Psalms portrays this journey in gripping ways.

When I begin to press my students to think about how we envision the Psalter, I often come to the image of pilgrimage. People today go on pilgrimages, journeys with a goal in mind, a particular purpose. Ancient Israel went on pilgrimage to the temple to worship. The Psalms reflect that experience. In the introductory poems, the divine gift of life is front and center but still opposed by the pesky enemies. They and the trouble and woe of life continue to press the worshiping community until at the end of Book III in Ps 89 life as this community has known it as the Davidic kingdom comes to an end. There is no more king and thus justice and no more temple and thus atonement. The center has fallen, and the pressing question is where the giver of life is now. How can the community go forward in the midst of such chaos and rubble? The answer comes soon in Book IV. Before there was a kingdom or a David, the community had a king: YHWH. Beginning with Ps 93, the Psalter stunningly celebrates the reign of YHWH and calls the community therefore to sing a new song, for King YHWH will make possible a full and faithful life in this changed reality. With such a confession of faith, the pilgrimage moves in due time to the full-throated praise of God in Ps 150, that great symphony of praise for all of creation because of God's great deeds. Let everything that breathes praise King YHWH. When we with attention overhear the pilgrimage of faith to which the Psalter bears witness, it teaches us prayer; it sings worship; and it confesses our faith.

I increasingly come to think that the gathering of the book of Psalms is closely tied to the crisis of exile and its aftermath beginning with the fall of Jerusalem to the Babylonians in the sixth century BCE. That is indicated in the account I have just repeated of the story reflected in the book of Psalms as a whole. It is important to see that the confession "the Lord reigns" is no abstract theory or some frothy confession to make the community feel better. Not the king of Babylon or of Persia or of the Greco-Roman Empire, but YHWH rules. That is a hard-won reality in the midst of a world with no center, a world with chaos knocking at the door and perhaps even flooding through the windows. I would suggest that we could characterize our world with the same language.

One of the reasons I suggest this perspective is that the story of the book of Psalms as a whole is not a one-dimensional narrative moving from plea to praise. In Books IV and V of the Hebrew Psalter also are texts that protest to God about the rubble and chaos that characterized their world. Psalm 102 cries for God to rebuild the ruins of Zion. The parade examples of imprecatory psalms come in Pss 109 and 137. The pilgrimage Songs of Ascents in Pss 120–134 are keenly aware of the dangers of the pilgrimage of faith; even the beautiful and moving Ps 139 concludes with the loathing of malicious enemies. And the last Davidic collection in the Psalter, Pss 138–145, includes a strong presence of lament. A number of these psalms reflect a tradition running back much earlier in the Psalter of protest, especially protest of the devastating experience of exile and its aftermath. We are probably more familiar with the view of the fall of Jerusalem that dominates the Former Prophets: the devastation is the result of the community's covenant faithlessness. Psalms 44; 74; 79; 89; 102; and the moving and bone-chilling Ps 137 powerfully articulate the underbelly of that dialogue of faith and in troubling language reflect the faithful post-Holocaust tradition of protest: God, where are you? How long? Have you completely wiped us from your memory? That arresting tradition of protest linked with the amazing celebration of the reign of YHWH leads to my last comment.

CONCLUSION

The stance of faith articulated by the Psalter as a whole is remarkably challenging for people and communities of faith. In reading the Psalter, we are in one sense eavesdropping on the prayers of the psalmists, but these texts invite more. They call us to enter the pilgrimage they imagine, with its mix of intellect and emotion, celebration and questioning, instruction and protest.

We are challenged both to confess with enthusiasm that the Lord reigns and to protest with Ps 89:

> How long, O LORD? Will you hide yourself forever? (v. 46a)
> ....
> LORD, where is your steadfast love of old? (v. 49b)

This chapter has focused, however, on the praise of God in the grammar of faith in the declarative and descriptive psalms. They narrate and describe in gripping images the God who comes to deliver and is present to bless and speaks to guide. This experience of divine sovereignty and persistent love provides a central plank of the grammar. Praise and lament are at the heart of the grammar of faith that is the book of Psalms. The Psalter is true to life, one of the reasons it is such a powerful resource for faith. It calls us to stand in a place holding together all the parts of the anatomy of the human soul. It is in a sense Luther's "little Bible" as it confesses our faith, our prayer, and our worship. I am reminded of George W. Anderson's phrasing: "Israel's creed sung, not signed."[21] Who could ask for more?

4

THE SHAPE OF THE GRAMMAR

A Proposal

This project characterizes the Psalter as a grammar of faith focusing on prayer and worship, and suggests reading the Psalms as a purposeful collection tied to issues related to theodicy. That is to say that this grammar of faith comes to us wrapped in a particular literary context, and that context shapes how we receive the grammar. I was educated as a form critic and biblical theologian. The first three chapters of this volume pursue those traditional issues of Psalms scholarship from a contemporary setting. The tasks of form criticism continue to offer much to interpreters of the Psalms, but the context in which we now work is rather different than it was when I began to work on these texts more than four decades ago. The broader field of literary criticism has influenced methods of biblical interpretation, an influence that offers much to those of us interested in the poetry and theology of the Psalter. One aspect of that influence is attention to *Sitz in der Literatur* (setting in literature—in the book of Psalms as a whole), along with concerns of *Gattung* (literary type) and *Sitz im Leben* (setting in life, usually cultic). I have introduced questions of the context of the book of Psalms as a whole in the previous chapters, and I pursue such literary approaches in this chapter.[1] I will begin by bringing together the history of scholarship that falls under the rubric of "the shape and shaping of the Psalter." Then I will give particular attention to the recent work of David Willgren and suggest a way forward. I will illustrate the possibilities with attention to the five books of the Psalter and to the shape of the Psalter as a whole and implications of this approach. The shape of the Psalter provides the literary context for the grammar of faith; it presents the grammar in a particular guise and with particular directions for reflection and interaction with readers. The shape of the Psalter is thus essential to learning the grammar.

History of Scholarship

What is often called "the shape and shaping of the Psalter" as an interpretive approach in recent scholarship goes back to the canonical reading strategy of Brevard S. Childs and, in particular, his Old Testament introduction.[2] He points to various emphases in the shape of the book of Psalms in the Christian canon, such as the introductory function of Ps 1. A predecessor of Childs' work was Westermann's essay on the formation of the book of Psalms, first published in 1962 and included in his *Praise and Lament in the Psalms*.[3] He suggests that an earlier collection was framed by the wisdom Pss 1 and 119, to which smaller collections were added. He also notes that the Psalter moves from lament to praise and from individual to community. I think most interpreters would agree that the canonical collection of 150 psalms came together by collections, with the Davidic collections at the core initially, followed by the Korahite and Asaphite collections.

The work that shifted the direction of Psalms study toward attention to the book of Psalms as a whole was Gerald Wilson's Yale dissertation *The Editing of the Hebrew Psalter*.[4] David Willgren has recently claimed that Wilson's work reshaped the conversation in Psalms study.[5] Wilson examines other ancient poetic collections and then looks at how the Hebrew Psalter is organized into its five books. He argues that Books I–III (Pss 1–89) have a different editorial history than do Books IV–V. He suggests that the first three books reflect the Davidic monarchy from its initiation (Ps 2) to its demise (Ps 89). Books IV–V reassert the kingship of YHWH as a basis for the community to go forward in a postexilic context without a Davidic monarch. Wilson's interpretive direction has been pursued by a number of scholars. McCann understands Ps 2 to focus on the reign of YHWH rather than the Davidic monarchy and interprets other royal and enthronement psalms to provide "an eschatological orientation" for the Psalter, particularly in the harsh aftermath of exile.[6] McCann's view understands the messianic functions to be democratized among the community. We will see in the discussion of the beginning of the Psalter below that Mays and deClaissé-Walford also point to Pss 1–2 as providing direction for interpretation with their emphases on torah and the reign of YHWH.[7]

Mitchell, among others, has claimed that Wilson does not do justice to the Davidic elements present in Books IV and V.[8] Snearly has suggested that the textual return of David implies an eschatological expectation in the latter parts of the Psalter. Snearly interprets the Psalter as a narrative unity with a storyline. He revises Wilson's interpretation of Ps 89 "as a lament over the present, shameful state of the Davidic dynasty, yet hope remains that Yahweh's covenant loyalty will reverse this deplorable condition."[9] Book IV highlights the sovereign reign of YHWH. Concerning Book V, Snearly summarizes:

> There is a purposeful arrangement of psalm groups in Book V and that this arrangement should be interpreted as signaling a renewed hope in the royal/ Davidic promises. Each psalm group of Book V is organized around a theme or key word that is related to the royal/Davidic hope in the earlier sections of the Psalter.[10]

Book V bears witness in the aftermath of exile to "a future expectation that Yahweh would display an eternal covenant loyalty to David by sending a king like David to consummately fulfill all of Yahweh's purpose."[11]

Brueggemann emphasizes torah in his reading of the Psalter as a whole.[12] He understands the introductory psalm to suggest reading the Psalter through the vision of torah obedience. Eventually the Psalter moves from obedience to covenant relationship with God to trust as reflected in the full-throated praise of God at the end of the Psalter. He suggests that the decisive turning point in the book comes in Ps 73 at the beginning of Book III, where the predominance of lament leads to a crisis of faith based on torah obedience. Obedience to torah has not brought justice to life. Creach suggests that refuge in YHWH as central to the destiny of the righteous provides central themes to the Psalter as a whole.[13] Erich Zenger has made a particular contribution to the interpretation of the fifth book of Psalms.[14] He notes the connections of the fifth book of Psalms to Zion and the temple but also the absence of concrete references to the cult. He suggests that the book is recited as a spiritual pilgrimage to the seat of the universal ruler, YHWH, who teaches torah from Zion. The praise of God in this concluding book of the Psalter comes in the midst of trouble and woe. The work of Zenger and Frank-Lothar Hossfeld makes important contributions in this stream of Psalms studies.[15] They attend to the various stages of formation of the book of Psalms, and so their approach is more redactional in nature (shaping) but with attention to literary contexts. They consider lexical and thematic links between psalms. Their conclusions about the resulting shape of the Psalter have some similarities to Wilson's, though they arrive at the conclusions in different ways. The end of the Psalter relates to its beginning and suggests a postcultic *Sitz im Leben* for the encounter with the divine in the book itself.

Two additional works attend to the connections between individual psalms. Matthias Millard suggests the clusters of psalms that make up the five books,[16] and David M. Howard works on the linguistic and thematic connections between individual psalms.[17] This last work concentrates on the microstructure level. Most of the other studies noted concentrate on the macrostructure level. Some of the studies focus on the shaping of the Psalter, that is, on issues of redaction and editing. Some focus on the shape of the Psalter, that is, the literary design of the book as a whole. I am more interested in the latter focus, though the two are not unrelated. The phrase "the shape and shaping of the Psalter" includes both. We need also to attend to those who are critical of this approach to study of the Psalms. Of particular note are the works of Norman Whybray and Erhard Gerstenberger. Whybray suggests that the answers to the shape of the "book" have been too varied to inspire confidence.[18] Gerstenberger presses on with a form-critical approach, locating the *Sitz im Leben* in a synagogal setting.[19] That liturgical setting accounts for the need to collect the Psalms rather than a literary motivation.

So how might we move forward with this stream of scholarship? In terms of the shape of the Psalter, Wilson's proposal as the groundbreaking publication continues to have considerable influence. There are some notable variations and some works that focus on the connections between individual psalms, but most of those concerned with the shape of the Psalter understand Pss 1–2 as introductory and as introducing the themes of torah and kingship. The place of Book III and especially its conclusion in Ps 89 as the demise or low point of Davidic rule is also important to the sequence of the Psalter. The place of Books IV and V is less clear. The movement is toward hope, but is it a hope tied to Davidic promises or to a different kind of future for the community of YHWH's people? Implicit in this summary is the suggestion that those who attend to the literary design of the Hebrew Psalter understand the context of its shape to be the crisis of exile and its aftermath. We will return to this perspective. This brief sketch of the movement of scholarship also makes clear that questions remain.[20]

This summary account of the literary design of the Psalter suggests an approach much in line with the approach of poetics, the careful study of texts as literature with attention to artistic aspects and their impact on readers. At the center is how texts communicate. Readers make sense of texts by attending to textual clues and transforming those clues in the hermeneutical process.[21] Texts invite readers into the process of interaction, leading to construction of meaning. Some would suggest that readers create meaning,[22] but I suggest that the production of meaning happens somewhere in the interaction between texts and informed readers. Poetics emphasizes the textual clues. One of the important clues literary critics note is the sequencing of texts. The beginnings of texts often have lasting impact in the interpretation of texts; it is labeled the primacy effect. The recency effect suggests that subsequent clues may lead readers to change interpretive directions. Scholars who attend to the book of Psalms as a whole suggest that the sequencing of texts put together in a collection in the same way provides important interpretive clues. The scribes who shaped the Hebrew Psalter did so with goals in mind for communicating with readers. Their ordering of the poetic texts is one of the rhetorical strategies to persuade readers. We will continue to explore the direction of that persuasive purpose.

A RECENT PROPOSAL

Willgren has recently published *The Formation of the "Book" of Psalms*.[23] The word "book" is in quotations in the title because Willgren takes the view that this anachronistic term is inappropriate for the Psalter. It does not fit the scribal culture from which the collection of psalms derives. His starting point is that Wilson's 1985 volume shifted the direction of Psalms study from the form-critical consensus of Gunkel and Mowinckel. Willgren finds the various proposals for the shape of the book to be incomplete and thus unconvincing. He proposes that the label of anthology is more appropriate for this collection of poetry. He spends some time defining and characterizing anthologies. He ties the etymology of the term to the gathering of flowers, and his definition is "a compilation of independent texts, actively selected and organized in relation to some present needs, inviting readers to a platform of continuous dialogue."[24] He suggests that anthologies can be seen as means for preserving, transmitting, and creating tradition. I think we can see the similarities to canon formation.

Willgren then considers ancient anthologies and particularly reconsiders the Qumran material. He comes to the view that there was not a two-stage stabilization process for the Psalter as proposed by Sanders, Flint, and Wilson.[25] There was no set sequencing of psalms. That seems to fit the ancient character of anthologies. What leads readers of anthologies is what Willgren labels "paratexts" in the tradition of Gérard Genette, artificial markers in the collection to give it some organization. Such paratexts would be prefaces, titles, colophons, doxologies, and epilogues. I think we can see the connection to the Psalms, and Willgren then pursues each of those as well as texts that are repeated. He puts all these things together in a reconstruction of the formation of the Psalter, closing in the second century BCE. He then concludes with why the collection was formed. It preserves the tradition of psalms that have stood the test of time, but Willgren argues that ancient anthologies and their paratexts do not suggest one purpose or suggest reading the anthologies as a whole. Rather, he understands the anthology of the Psalms to be a multivocal work with a powerful selection of psalms that present the ongoing interaction between God and community.

I find Willgren's proposal to be both interesting and important, and I want to pursue several of its dimensions though in some cases from quite different perspectives. First to the matter of the Psalter as an anthology. I think most of us think of anthologies as simply collections of compositions, often from a variety of authors, with perhaps some organization but most often collections like pearls on a string with little focus to the whole. Willgren's definition suggests that the selection and organization of the collection invites readers to a conversation. When one enters a garden of flowers, the anthology invites one to look at the various flowers and, no doubt, to enjoy some more than others. The garden includes paths, signs, and fences to guide visitors in various directions. The paratexts provide structure for readers but do not dictate only one way to walk through the garden.[26] I think Willgren seeks to recover for us a much more robust characterization of anthologies. In this sense, I think it helpful to think of the Hebrew Psalter as an anthology. It provides a way for readers to attend to both individual psalms and the collection of psalms as a whole, just as I would characterize the Psalter as both songbook and prayer book. The label of *anthology* provides more flexibility to those of us who seek to make sense of the Psalter as a whole. One of the ways in which I differ from Willgren is that I am still strongly influenced by Wilson's proposal. At the same time, not any of the proposals for the "message" of the book of Psalms completely convinces me. The Psalter seems sufficiently diverse so that its messaging is, by design, varied. I think particularly of the lengthy and multivocal fifth book of Psalms. It suggests to me a considerable variety of narratives for readers to pursue. It does not move in only one direction but in several.

At the same time, there are several ways in which I would dissent from Willgren's bold proposal. I have already mentioned a more positive response to Wilson. I am also still convinced by the consensus views of psalm superscriptions and their indications of collections included in the Psalter as well as more standard understandings of the formation of the Hebrew Psalter. Of particular importance is the matter of the significance of the sequence of psalms. Willgren has not, as he fully admits, attended to many of the linguistic and thematic connections between psalms. Because of his understanding of the formation of the Psalter, he does not attribute a lot of significance to the sequence of psalms in the collection. Interpreters from the broader field of literary criticism often suggest that the sequencing of texts is one of the important clues for readers. Beginnings, for example, often create a primacy effect that influences the production of meaning. How a text continues brings adjustments to interpretation. That is true of individual texts and, I suggest, is also true of the sequencing of poems in an anthology such as the Psalter. The very process of reading suggests that the sequencing of texts is an important interpretive clue. Psalms are discrete poems, and they so often lead the reader to the next poem. Willgren objects to the interpretive tradition of *Sitz in der Literatur* because it does not fit his understanding of the scribal culture from which the Psalter arose.[27] Here surfaces a crucial difference between my hermeneutic and Willgren's. My goal is not to follow interpretive paths that fit the historical context from which the Psalter arose but to articulate ways of reading the Psalter that provide clues for readers to appropriate these texts in profound ways. Do not misunderstand. I fully believe that the cultural codes of the originating social context are woven into the Psalms, though we are frequently not privy to the knowledge of how that process happened. At the same time, I understand the production of meaning to take place in a conversation between texts and readers. Textual clues invite readers to make sense of these signals and bring the meaning to fruition. It is the productive interaction between text and reader that is essential to my literary and theological hermeneutic, and by readers I mean informed readers, both ancient and contemporary.[28] Given this hermeneutical understanding, the shape of the Hebrew Psalter necessarily provides readers with an important interpretive context.

So, in summary, I understand the Psalter as an anthology of considerable import. It preserves canonical liturgical poetry. It also provides a context for interpretation. I am following the analogy of paths, signs, and fences in a garden of flowers. The context is central to the grammar of faith to which the Psalter bears witness. We now need to suggest the shape of that context. I do so by way of the five-book organization of the Hebrew Psalter.

Book I

Most scholars who attend to the shape and shaping of the Psalter agree that the first two psalms serve introductory purposes.[29] Both psalms appear without superscriptions, an unusual occurrence in Book I of the Psalter. The first psalm begins with *'ašrê* (blessed/happy/whole); the term reappears at the end of Ps 2, a clue to read the two poems together. The psalms do not comprise one text, but they do appear to be connected and function as a double introduction to the book.[30] The reference in Ps 1:2 to the instruction or direction of YHWH which is to be meditated upon day and night suggests reading the Psalter as instruction for the community of faith. I suggest that Ps 1 gathers the participants in the Psalter that now begins to unfold: YHWH, the righteous, and their opponents the wicked. These opponents persist in Book I. As we read on to Ps 2, the enemies persist and become the nations who oppose YHWH and YHWH's anointed. The psalm concludes by urging the rulers of these nations to submit to divine authority and thereby encounter divine refuge. When readers continue to Ps 3, enemies surround David, according to the superscription and the psalm's opening verse. And enemies persist as we read on in the first several psalms.

Reading Pss 1–2 as a double introduction to the Psalter is based in recent Psalms scholarship. It goes back to the work of Childs on canonical readings of biblical texts: "Psalm 1 has assumed a highly significant function as a preface to the psalms which are to be read, studied, and meditated upon."[31] The connection to torah in Ps 1 suggests that connection for the Psalter it introduces. Wilson pursues this perspective for the first psalm.[32] Brueggemann suggests that the first psalm leads to reading the Psalms from the perspective of torah obedience.[33] McCann moves the conversation to Ps 2, which he interprets in terms of the reign of YHWH and an eschatological perspective. It offers hope in the troubles that persist in the aftermath of exile.[34] So for McCann, the Psalter portrays the reign of YHWH—present though opposed—and the community's response in faithful living. DeClaissé-Walford reads the Psalter as a whole by way of the emphases on torah and divine rule in Pss 1–2.[35] Miller's interpretation of the first two psalms as the beginning of the Psalter emphasizes torah and the king under threat.[36]

I agree with Miller that the introductory psalms reveal two voices: the person who lives by torah (the *'îš* [individual] of Ps 1:1) and the king under threat. Those voices never leave the frame of Book I. Additional royal texts are Pss 18; 20; 21, and note the superscriptions to Pss 3; 7; 18; 34; 36. I would suggest that the more pervasive poetic voice, however, is that of the *'îš* who resists the advice of the wicked and attends to the guidance of torah. I have already suggested that this wise or righteous one attends to the direction of the Psalter, more particularly the psalms of Book I as a school of prayer in the face of persistent enemies. While I have characterized the teaching of the first book somewhat differently, Creach also interprets Book I "as an extended picture of true piety."[37]

The clusters of psalms in Book I illustrate this perspective. Psalms 3–14 focus on model prayers of lament in settings of trouble and opposition.[38] Psalm 8 is a hymn of praise, but the vow concluding Ps 7 leads to this praise and indeed the beginning of Ps 9 also echoes that concluding vow.[39]

> I will give to the LORD the thanks due to his righteousness,
> and sing praise to the name of the LORD, the Most High. (Ps 7:17)

> I will give thanks to the LORD with my whole heart;
> I will tell of all your wonderful deeds.
> I will be glad and exult in you;
> I will sing praise to your name, O Most High. (Ps 9:1-2)

A shift takes place with Ps 15, where torah becomes explicit, here torah on worship. Psalms 15–24 comprise the next cluster of psalms.[40] Psalm 19, at the center of this cluster, focuses on torah. This group of psalms solidifies the first book's connection to instruction. The instruction is very much in the context of worship, with the worship emphases of Pss 15 and 24 and the superscriptions of Pss 30 and 38. These first two clusters of psalms confirm the umbrella of a grammar of faith as a way of meditating upon the prayer and worship modeled in the first book of the Psalter. Models for prayer and praise are at the heart of the next cluster of Pss 25–34. Praise is for the God who brings hope in the midst of trouble and woe. Prayer in the face of enemies again comes to the fore with the final cluster of Pss 35–41 in Book I. The book's concluding psalm echoes Ps 1 with the affirmation that while enemies persist, so does the blessing of divine presence.

So the shape of Book I of the Hebrew Psalter includes the double introduction of Pss 1–2 and four clusters (Pss 3–14; 15–24; 25–34; 35–41). The emphases in these texts suggest a grammar of faith centered on prayer and worship in the life of the community. A transparent covenant dialogue is present in these model prayers. Prayer here is honest to God. Prayer here is also sung in the context of worship and so is heard by all the community. Prayer has a community dimension. So prayer is here wrestling with both God and the community and operates in a context of hope.

I have elsewhere suggested that the introductory psalms have a primacy effect on readers of Book I and of the Psalter as a whole.[41] These introductory psalms set the themes to come. There are various parts to the collection in Book I, as befits the first section of an anthology. A direction for the various parts is, however, discernible. The poetic texts articulate a grammar of faith centered on prayer and worship for the community. The texts thus instruct readers. While the royal voice never goes away entirely, the primary voice is that of the faithful *'iš* who attends to the divine instruction. Another theme detectable in the poetry is the call to take refuge in YHWH. An anthology provides space for a diversity of themes. These poems articulate a grammar of faith and thus teach that faith, as suggested by the introductory psalms.

Book II

Book II moves readers in its witness to a grammar of faith past the first Davidic collection of psalms. Psalms 42–49 bring readers of the Hebrew Psalter to the psalms of the guild of Korah, a Levite and leader of this guild of psalmists (1 Chr 9:19; 2 Chr 20:19). Most commentators take Pss 42–43 as originally one text. This individual prayer opens Book II and is followed by a community lament. While these psalms likely arose in different contexts, the literary setting in Book II may well relate to the ancient community's trauma of exile and especially the trauma of the destruction of Jerusalem as a sacred place of divine presence. The opening prayer certainly keys on the journey of exile, whether in terms of place or spirit. The psalm moves toward the hope of encounter with the divine in the sanctuary with the worshiping community. The powerful community lament in Ps 44 focuses on YHWH's covenant default in the face of the community's covenant obedience.

> All this has come upon us,
> yet we have not forgotten you,
> or been false to your covenant.
> . . . .
> Because of you we are being killed all day long,
> and accounted as sheep for the slaughter. (Ps 44:17, 22)

The royal Ps 45 is more hopeful. Psalms 46, 47, and 48 all focus on divine rule. Psalms 46 and 48 celebrate YHWH's choice of Zion as the place of the divine dwelling. Psalm 47 shapes the liturgical celebration of divine rule. The concluding psalm of this Korahite collection (Ps 49) takes the form of wisdom instruction and argues that it is the relationship with the divine, rather than riches, that brings life. The Korahite collection opens Book II with a context of lament for both individual and community and in a context of exile and defeat. That perspective is in tension with the affirmations of divine rule in the psalms that follow. This sequence of psalms at the beginning of Book II also reveals connections with the opening sequence of Book III and suggests that the experience of exile may undergird the editorial shape of the collections.⁴² The Korahite collection concludes with an emphasis on divine presence, rather than worldly success, as the goal. This Korahite collection is also part of the Elohistic Psalter named for the dominant divine name used rather than YHWH. The overlapping collections signal the process of collecting that issued in the Hebrew Psalter's five books and 150 psalms.

Psalm 50 is a psalm of Asaph and is something of an outlier since the collection of Psalms of Asaph begins Book III (Pss 73–83). This psalm provides a bridge between the Korahite collection and the collection of Davidic psalms beginning with Ps 51. The divine presence marked in the Korahite psalms now in Zion speaks to the community with an emphasis on covenant renewal.

The next collection of Davidic psalms begins with the familiar penitential lament Ps 51.

> Fifteen psalms of David appear in the middle of Book Two (Psalms 51–65). Fourteen of them are laments. Eight are connected, in their superscriptions, with particular events in the life of David. These psalms remind readers once again that David's life was one of turmoil and strife; but they also depict for readers a king who loved the Lord and strove to serve the Lord with great fervor.⁴³

The editorial superscriptions suggest to readers that they read these prayers along with the referenced Davidic narratives. These narratives relate to a lived context of faith and portray David as not the grand and glorious king but as the struggling person of faith. Just as David faced persistent opposition, so enemies are at the forefront in these laments. Their pernicious presence is a major theme in these Davidic psalms. The depth of the complaint and the transparency of plea in this part of Book II are painful. Beginning with Ps 60, the collection suggests a mood of deeper trust in YHWH. Psalm 65 offers praise to the creator. These texts and their superscriptions are all part of the grammar of faith to which the Psalter bears witness with its modeling of passionate and transparent prayer.

Psalms 66–67 focus on thanksgiving both public and personal. The psalms include superscriptions but do not name David. The name of David appears again with Pss 68–71. Psalm 68 celebrates the God of our salvation. Additional laments follow. Psalm 71 is without superscription, but it has a number of connections with Ps 70 and thus can be considered along with its predecessor.⁴⁴ Psalm 72 concludes Book II with a prayer carrying the name of Solomon in its superscription. It is a prayer for the righteous king and so could perhaps be understood as "for Solomon." It also indicates that the figure of David will now recede to the background as "the prayers of David son of Jesse are ended" (v. 20). Verses 18-20 provide the traditional benediction for the book.

Book III

Book III plays a pivotal role in the shape of the Hebrew Psalter; it is the middle plate of a pentad and so provides readers with essential interpretive clues, key emphases of the grammar. The book begins with a collection of Psalms of Asaph (Pss 73–83) followed by another collection of Korahite Psalms (Pss 84–88, interrupted by a Davidic psalm in Ps 86) and concludes with the lengthy and important royal Ps 89. Asaph is listed as a temple musician in 1 Chr 15:17-19; 16:4-5; Ezra 3:10. This organization of Book III suggests that the sequence of the anthology is moving in the direction of an emphasis on the impact of exile and defeat for this community. The themes present in the Psalms of Asaph make it clear that things have changed considerably following the hopeful prayer for the king at the end of Book II. The grammar is tied to the community's life experience.

Psalm 73 is a reflection on the difficult questions of theodicy from one who is troubled by the prosperity of the wicked. The gathering effect of the dominance of individual laments in Books I and II reaches a pivot with this theodical wisdom poem tinged with lament. It has become clear that living rightly does not bring prosperity. The psalm moves from issues related to the pursuit of commodities to hope found in communion with the divine in the worshiping community. The key shift comes in v. 17 with entrance into the sanctuary, a fundamental move in the Psalter's grammar of faith:

until I went into the sanctuary of God . . .

The experience there brings the move from concern about prosperity to concern about the divine presence; true refuge is found in God. Psalm 74 also vividly narrates a crisis, this time for the community. That crisis is made all the more profound with the connection to Ps 73, for this community lament powerfully portrays the destruction of the sanctuary, where the speaker in the first psalm of the collection found hope in the midst of trouble. Now that sanctuary is in rubble. The psalm still affirms the divine rule but fervently pleads for a renewal of covenant in the face of devastation all around. The beginning of Ps 75 and its "wondrous deeds" echoes the conclusion of Ps 73 and bears witness to God's works that bring justice to the arrogant.

When reading Psalms 73–75 in sequence, one also realizes that Psalm 75 sounds like a response to the concluding section of Psalm 74 and its petitions. The question of divine rule and justice is at the core of these three psalms that begin this Asaphite collection. Psalm 75 affirms the divine justice. Many interpreters would tie this collection of psalms to a time related to exile.[45]

The emphasis on the wondrous deeds of the God in Zion continues in Ps 76. In Ps 77, this God remains faithful to the righteous in the face of trouble and woe. The lengthy historical recitation in Ps 78 continues to affirm the fidelity of God. Psalm 79 returns to the powerful memory of the destruction of Jerusalem. These psalms are conscious of the failings of the community but also struggle with faith in the reign of YHWH and divine fidelity to the covenant promises. Psalm 80 hopes for restoration, and Ps 81 focuses again on the place of memory in dealing with such a powerful crisis as now faces the worshiping community. The psalm features directive divine speech that reminds the people of the need for covenant faithfulness. Psalm 82 is unusual in that here YHWH calls for faithfulness even among the gods, and the faithfulness is demonstrated in justice. Psalm 83 concludes the Psalms of Asaph by raising issues of divine justice similar to those in Ps 73 that begin the collection. In the initial psalm the concern is about individuals; in the concluding psalm the concern is about the community. Psalms 82 and 83 conclude with the topic of divine rule over all the earth: "This theme of divine judgment characterizes the psalms of Asaph."[46]

The Psalms of Asaph and the Elohistic Psalter come to an end with Ps 83. Psalms 84–85 and 87–88 constitute a second collection of Psalms of the Korahite guild. Psalm 84, a Zion song, brings to mind the beginning of the Korahite collection in Book II (Pss 42–43) with the yearning to encounter the divine presence in worship. Psalm 85 seeks restoration for the community. Psalm 86 interrupts the Korahite psalms with a Davidic lament. Psalm 87 returns to the theme of Zion, followed by one of the most powerful individual laments in Scripture. Psalm 88 is an unrelenting prayer in the midst of the sojourn in Sheol that simply ends in "darkness." There is no word of hope at the end.[47] Transparency in the grammar of prayer is clear and present. This overwhelming lament leads to the concluding psalm in Book III, a vivid royal lament. The text begins with a lengthy recounting of the Davidic covenant promise that the descendants of David would rule over Jerusalem as the line chosen by YHWH. Now the kingdom has fallen (vv. 38-45). This defeat and exile even raise the question of the presence of the divine persistent love (ḥesed) and faithfulness ('emet) at the end of the psalm. Transparency abounds in this prayer, this articulation of the relationship of people and God.

Book III has struggled with the justice of the divine reign. By the end of the book, the question has risen to the very heart of all covenant relationships in the Hebrew Scriptures: Is the divine persistent love (*ḥesed*) to be trusted? Book III is clearly dealing with theodical issues raised by defeat and exile encountered in the sixth century. That concern becomes explicit in the concluding psalm of the book. The book ends with a one-line benediction: "Blessed be the Lord forever. Amen and Amen" (v. 52). The psalms in Book III struggle, and in some ways alternate between, confessions of faith in YHWH, the God of Zion, and in searing questions of divine justice and divine fidelity. The tone focuses on distress. The enemy from the north is oppressive; the community seeks to glean hope from its memories of other times of distress, looking again to memories of exodus, wilderness, and entry into the land. Psalm 78 makes clear that such memories also include divine judgment, and in Ps 81 God directly warns the community about covenant faithfulness in the form of an oracle. The psalms of praise near the end of the book focus on Jerusalem and Zion, but the two concluding psalms of the book raise questions about the divine presence for both individuals and community. Both psalms end with questions unresolved. Most scholars who attend to the shape of the Hebrew Psalter would agree that the shape of Book III is determined by the experience of defeat and exile. The dire crisis has brought the community to the edge of the unthinkable. That historical moment is very present in this central book of the Psalter. Beth Tanner articulates this understanding of Book III, but she also suggests that this section of the Psalter is not limited to that historical referent.[48]

> Book Three represents every time when the world and its violence make no sense, times when we do not understand why God does not simply fix it. Book Three is a poetic rendering of theodicy, and its themes fit as well today as they did in its ancient context.[49]

The Psalter's grammar persistently interacts with lived reality, and it does so in ways still present to contemporary communities of faith. This grammar continues to articulate the relationship between the divine and the human community. The shape of the anthology suggests that kind of direction for readers.

Book IV

Scholars who attend to the literary design of the Hebrew Psalter often point to the conclusion of Book III as a pivotal point. I do take the latter parts of

Ps 89 to suggest the end of the Davidic covenant and Davidic monarchy in the sixth century BCE.

> But now you have spurned and rejected him;
> you are full of wrath against your anointed.
> You have renounced the covenant with your servant;
> you have defiled his crown in the dust. (vv. 38-39)

Immediately following this conclusion of the third book, Book IV begins with a cluster of psalms that return to the theme of divine refuge. This cluster of Pss 90–92 seems to reflect back on ancient Israel's experience of exile. It is noteworthy that Ps 90 is the only psalm of Moses, according to the superscription, taking readers back to the time before the Davidic kingdom. It is also appropriate that Ps 90 is a community lament. This first cluster of psalms in Book IV includes themes of right perspective in the midst of trouble and woe.

Psalms 93–101 as the next cluster of psalms announce and explicate the theme of the reign of YHWH. Wilson understands these psalms as response to the fall of the Davidic kingdom at the end of Book III. McCann also labels these texts as the theological heart of the Psalter.[50] The hopeful announcement of divine rule calls for the community to sing a new song, for hope, justice, and faithfulness are possible even in the face of the despair of exile still surrounding the community. Psalm 94 concludes with an affirmation of divine refuge in the midst of considerable opposition. The affirmation of divine rule in the succeeding psalms suggests that YHWH has not forgotten ḥesed for the community (Ps 98:3). The celebration of the divine rule suggests that the world is different with YHWH as ruler and that the chaos of exile will not obliterate a way forward for the community of YHWH. The familiar call to worship the divine king in Ps 100 forms a fitting conclusion to the collection of enthronement psalms celebrating the reign of YHWH. Following is the royal, Davidic Ps 101, often interpreted as a kind of "oath of office" from the Davidic king. It may, however, be the case that with the question put in v. 2, the psalm is an articulation of insistent hope for a just order, a sign of divine rule.[51] This cluster of psalms is at the heart of the Psalter's grammar.

Psalms 102–106 comprise the final cluster of psalms in Book IV. They call the community to come to terms with the haunting crisis of exile in the context of the affirmation of divine rule. The texts affirm YHWH as creator and redeemer still even in the midst of community trauma. Ancient Israel is once again in the wilderness, as in the time of Moses, but now as a consequence of exile. The hope is that the community can imagine again by way of this articulated grammar the reign of YHWH and forge a life together even in the midst of defeat. The book's concluding psalm suggests the cry of confession as a means to the divine *ḥesed* that is still possible. The concluding plea of Ps 106, just before the doxology for Book IV, reflects the setting:

> Save us, O LORD our God,
> and gather us from among the nations,
> that we may give thanks to your holy name
> and glory in your praise. (v. 47)

BOOK V

The lengthy Book V (Pss 107–150) continues from the conclusion of Ps 106. The book begins with words of thanksgiving to God for deliverance from exile in Babylon and return home.

> Let the redeemed of the LORD say so,
> those he redeemed from trouble
> and gathered in from the lands,
> from the east and from the west,
> from the north and from the south. (Ps 107:2-3)

Persian policy allowed a return to Jerusalem and a rebuilding of the temple, though the community was now part of a province in the Persian Empire. The wisdom-tinged conclusion of the opening psalm of the final book (vv. 42-43) puts these events in the context of YHWH's *ḥesed* and provides a context for the remainder of the book. Psalm 107 opens the grammar of the book.

Book V consists of several clusters of psalms: 107–110; 111–118; 119; 120–137; 138–145; 146–150: "This final collection can be seen as a representative smorgasbord of many of the psalms that have come before."[52] Psalm 107 provides several case studies in the community's thanksgiving for divine deliverance from troubles. Psalms 108–110 complete the first cluster of psalms and all carry the name of David in their superscriptions. Psalm 108 combines materials from Pss 57 and 60 and continues the tone of thanksgiving in Book V.[53] Psalm 109 is a parade example of an individual imprecatory psalm. Psalm 110 is a royal text that at least suggests some kind of hope for the future of this community.

The acrostic Pss 111–112 celebrate God's mighty acts and call for a response by way of torah. These psalms introduce the Hallel that follows in Pss 113–118. The title comes from the verb used in the call to praise "Hallelujah." This collection of psalms is associated with Passover. These psalms praise the incomparable Lord who brought Israel out of Egypt. Psalm 115 emphasizes the contrast between YHWH and the idols other people have made; this concern fits the context of Book V in dealing with the crisis of exile and its aftermath and provides an important tenet of the Psalter's historical grammar. The "cup of salvation" in Ps 116:13 provides a context for the recitation of the mighty acts of God in the Passover ritual. Psalm 118 is a fitting conclusion to this collection with use of the divine *hesed* and of the call to praise, Hallelujah. The psalm bases the call to praise on the exodus experience. The psalm also alludes to the opening psalm of Book V. God's past acts of deliverance for the community can be the basis for a future hope.[54]

Psalm 119 in some ways dominates the fifth book of psalms as a psalm cluster by itself. Its theme of torah brings to mind the opening of the Hallel in Pss 111–112. Torah is thus one of the themes of the fifth book. Torah is a means of responding to a generous God with fidelity and is thus central to the book's grammar of faith. The psalm is a centerpiece in the anthology.

The Songs of Ascents follow in Pss 120–134 as a collection of pilgrimage texts for those journeying to Jerusalem for worship. The psalms portray Jerusalem as the place for the community to gather for celebrations and for thanksgiving to God. Most of these texts are brief and relate to various dimensions of life brought into the remembered pilgrimage. The journey is not easy but brings the hope of blessing. The goal of the pilgrimage remembered in this collection is praise (Ps 134). Psalms 135–136 are appropriate postscripts to the Songs of Ascents, offering praise and thanksgiving. DeClaissé-Walford, Jacobson, and Tanner note that "some scholars suggest that Psalms 111–118 and Psalms 120–136 form an inclusion around the great Torah psalm 119."[55] Psalm 137 concludes the cluster. It fits awkwardly in this place but is tied to Zion and the yearning for Zion, though it is a bitter lament and an infamously imprecatory psalm.[56] It seems that exile continues as a present reality and context for the articulation of this grammar of faith. Psalm 137 punctuates the anthology with a historical memory.

Psalms 138–145 constitute the final Davidic collection of psalms. As with earlier Davidic collections, lament is very present. The prayers in this collection are closely intertwined and call to mind other Davidic prayers. The prayers have now been placed in this collection in Book V in a context tied to exile. Psalm 145 celebrates YHWH as ruler and calls the community to the celebration that shall be known to all people. It may well be that v. 21 serves as the concluding doxology for Book V, leading to the concluding texts for the Psalter. Such a hint of a benediction fits the nature of anthologies.

> My mouth will speak the praise of the LORD,
> and all flesh will bless his holy name forever and ever.

Psalms 146–150 serve as the fivefold concluding doxology to the Hebrew Psalter as the final Hallel, and the Psalter concludes with a stunning universal call to praise YHWH. The concluding psalms praise YHWH who reigns. The Psalter ends with an explosive call to praise.

> Let everything that breathes praise the LORD! Praise the Lord!

The reading community is called into worship and covenant fidelity in this part of its grammar. Book V begins with return from exile but understands that lament and questions are still very much present. The themes of divine reign and torah are very much present in these texts as they are in the Psalter's introductory Pss 1–2. In one sense, the historical community of the Psalter continues as exiles in the Persian Empire in a time of chaos and yet also in a new life with King YHWH. The Davidic kingdom is no more; the setting has changed but the sovereign YHWH still reigns and the community of YHWH's people still live with a past, present, and future: "Thus the Psalter is a story of survival in the changed and changing world that confronted the postexilic Israelite community of faith."[57] A grammar of faith is essential for the community in this new setting. The anthological character of the collection suggests that there is not one path ahead but paths with multiple narratives.

THEODICY

This brief account of the shape of the Psalter suggests that the issues the collection confronts stem from the crisis of exile and its aftermath. These questions move into the realm of theodicy, a topic both historical and contemporary. I suggest that the shape of the Psalter implies the hope of persuasive impact on reading communities concerned with this troubling issue. I do not take theodicy to be a narrow philosophical issue defined in only one way. I take any text dealing with evil and suffering in the world and divine justice to be a text dealing with theodical themes. A number of interpreters suggest that the Psalter was finally shaped sometime between the second century BCE and the first century CE.[58] I have suggested that the bulk of the shaping of the Psalter may well have been in place closer to the time of the return of some in the exilic community. Communities reading and hearing "the Hebrew Psalter in that era would still be confronting theodicy issues going back to the exile. More recent communities who would have received and read the Psalter would continue to stand in that tradition."[59]

The account above indicates that Book IV of the Psalter begins with a community lament to reflect back on the crisis of exile. Thus Ps 90 begins a response to the fall of Jerusalem and the Davidic kingdom at the end of Ps 89 and Book III. Central to that response is the collection of enthronement Pss 93–100. Psalm 93 announces the theme, and the psalms that follow take up various dimensions of the theme. The community looks for hope and justice in the faithfulness of a divine ruler and so hope to sing a new song in response to the reign of YHWH. The final cluster of psalms in Book IV seeks to help the reading community come to terms with the crisis of exile in the context of singing a new song of YHWH's reign. This reign is of old but now must find renewal in the community and in a new expression of its grammar of faith. The book begins with a psalm of Moses (Ps 90) to go back to a time before the Davidic kingdom. Even in the wilderness period, the community encountered the divine ruler's persistent love. The community is now in wilderness again after the fall of Jerusalem. It is called once again to imagine YHWH's reign even in such a chaotic time, and so is in need of a "new song," a new grammar of faith.

The reign of God is central to Book IV of the Psalter, and it is central to the Psalter as a whole. What Book IV does is place the theme squarely in the midst of the trauma of exile. These texts raise pressing issues of suffering and justice and evil, all in the midst of a central affirmation of the rule of YHWH. Book IV seeks to integrate hope in the reign of YHWH with the reality of exile, to put those two realities in conversation. Psalm 102 illustrates the point. The prayer begins with an individual lament emphasizing human frailty (vv. 1-11) in contrast to the reign of YHWH.

> But you, YHWH, sit enthroned forever
> and memory of you continues generation after generation. (v. 12, my translation)

That confession of faith is then placed precisely in the community's experience of exile in vv. 13-17. The prayer puts faith in the reign of YHWH in dialogue with the reality of exile. The hope is that the divine ruler will hear the cry of the community and deliver it from the crisis still at hand. The persistent dialogue with YHWH now includes the affirmation that YHWH reigns. The language of Book IV is not simply that of historical report but is persuasive language yearning for the help of the divine ruler and begging the community to imagine the hope this divine rule can bring. What a remarkable grammar of faith!

This hope of divine *ḥesed* in the midst of suffering is a theme that continues in Book V. The conclusion of Book IV in Ps 106:47 and the opening of Book V in Ps 107:1-3 suggest that the final book will relate to the community's suffering and difficulties in the aftermath of exile—the context of the grammar. The community searches for that persistent love to appear even in the midst of such trouble and woe. Psalm 107 opens the book with memories of how YHWH has brought persistent love to the community, and the book calls the community to imagine life with YHWH by reading the Psalter. Zenger has helpfully characterized Book V in terms of a "spiritual pilgrimage" to Zion as the place of YHWH's throne, YHWH who teaches torah. The concluding fivefold doxology of the Psalter sustains the confession of faith in the divine rule. The Psalter ends with an extended call to praise, a call to sing of the reign of YHWH, a kind of sung grammar.

Such an interpretive direction for Books IV and V is in line with various approaches to the pressing theological issue of theodicy. McCann speaks of the divine rule as both affirmed and opposed in the Psalter's poetry and proposes an eschatological perspective for the direction of the Psalter.[60] The not-yet-fulfilled character of divine rule provides one avenue for approaching such issues. Another emphasis is that the liturgical setting behind the enthronement psalms makes it possible for the community to imagine again the reign of YHWH. The new way of seeing life leads to a new song and a new language for hopeful living. That suggestion is more in line with Mowinckel's generative proposal for the *Sitz im Leben* of the enthronement psalms.[61] His enthronement festival celebrates the divine rule and thus calls the community to live into that hope even in the face of trouble and woe. Singing the new song encourages the beleaguered congregation to enact the song and thus help the reign of YHWH to become the reality it proclaims. This approach to Books IV and V supports the view that the trauma of exile persists in the shape of the Hebrew Psalter. That experience raised troubling questions for the community. In some cases, the response is in terms of the community's failure; thus confession of sin is the route prescribed. In other texts in the Psalter, the response is more in terms of protest than confession of sin. Indeed, the psalms of lament emphasize protest over confession most of the time and so present a provocative dimension to the grammar of faith. The anthology includes multiple directions.

Protest Songs

Our account of the shape of the Psalter suggests that Book III as the central panel in the pentad holds particular importance. Wilson understands the conclusion of Book III (Ps 89) to set the agenda for Books IV–V with the fall of the Davidic kingdom. How shall the community go forward after this devastating loss of what was seen as an expression of YHWH's ḥesed? I do think that the crisis of exile is very much present in Book III (Pss 73–89). The book begins with the Psalms of Asaph, and that collection begins with a reflection concerning the prosperity of the wicked, followed by a community lament over the fall of Jerusalem (see also Ps 79). The loss of the center in Zion colors the whole book. The Psalms of Asaph, however, continue to affirm the reign of YHWH as seen in the recital of the mighty acts of God. Both the transparent cries for justice from the people and the prophetic call for faithfulness are present in this collection. The Korahite psalms continue in the vein of lament that reaches a crescendo in the dark and accusing lament of Ps 88 and the plaintive royal lament that concludes the book with the fall of the Davidic kingdom and the search for YHWH's persistent love. The brutally honest grammar persists.

The anguished laments in Book III are part and parcel of the brutally honest dialogue of faith between Israel and YHWH. Such alarmingly honest prayers could well be labeled protest songs. Robert Cole has noted that the questions of "Why?" and "How long?" persist in this central book of the Psalter.[62] Enemies are present in these texts, but the central plot is the straightforward dialogue between Israel and YHWH. Theodicy here is no academic theological issue but literally a matter of life and death in the context of defeat and exile. A world rife with chaos is the context for these prayers of questions, and the community is to persist with such protests as their expressions of faith. The tradition of protest is not absent from Book IV with its laments (Pss 90, 94, 102, and 106).

> For we are consumed by your anger;
> By your wrath we are overwhelmed. (Ps 90:7)

In Book V the protest intensifies. Psalms 109 and 137 are the parade examples of individual and community psalms of imprecation.

> Help me, O Lord my God!
> Save me according to your steadfast love. (Ps 109:26)

> How could we sing the Lord's song
> in a foreign land? (Ps 137:4)

It is commonplace to note that laments dominate Books I and II of the Psalter, but they are also particularly intense near the conclusion of the Psalter.

Protest persists. Those who pray seek divine refuge in Pss 140–143. This approach of protest is a different way of dealing with issues tied to theodicy. The unrestrained covenant dialogue calls God to the task of bringing justice for the covenant community; it is a persistent grammar.

Questions of theodicy do not always take the traditional routes of Christian theology in the book of Psalms, but these questions pervade the book. The anthology leads readers to the questions and includes a variety of paths to follow but does not resolve the matter. That fits patterns of anthologies and keeps clarity that the Psalter does not resolve all questions. It rather invites worshipers into the liturgy of prayer and praise in the midst of questions. Indeed, the questions may well on occasion be the prayer and the confession of faith. The grammar of faith focuses on questions. The perspective of Ps 73:17 and the centrality of the sanctuary continue in the multifaceted anthology we call the book of Psalms. A literary reading of the Psalter as a whole by way of its sequences can help readers see the persuasive power of the Psalter on an interpretive community. While the anthology amply includes diverse directions, one of its central paths has to do with the living of theodical questions. The shape of the grammar gives a focus to the questions central to lived faith and so to the pilgrimage's directions.

5

THE MOVEMENT OF THE GRAMMAR

Directions for Readers

A FINAL TASK

This handbook has combined traditional Psalms scholarship—that is, form-critical work—with the more recent attention to the shape of the Psalter as a whole. In this last chapter, I am particularly interested in the implications of this work for understanding the organization of the latter parts of the Psalter. A grammar provides a structure for communicating. This grammar attends finally to the conversation between a life of faith and texts of psalms as well as the Psalter as a whole. Discrete psalms call for readers to continue the journey from reading into life. The same is true for the Psalter as a whole. For readers and hearers and singers and pray-ers of the Psalter, the movements of these latter sections suggest directions for faith beyond each individual reading of the book of Psalms. What do the concluding sections of the book of Psalms suggest to those who seek to converse with the book so that life and faith are enriched? I begin with a review of two of the important proposals about the shape of the Psalter and consider their implications. I then want to explore the poetics of Book V in relation to the form-critical categories of praise and lament. I will suggest that the shape of the Psalter includes multiple plot directions and that the praise of God at the end of the Psalter is part of a larger faith experience that includes lament. The goal is to engage something of the shape of the anthology and to integrate the Psalter into that faith experience. I begin with some history of scholarship.

History of Scholarship

In a forward-looking piece first published in 1962, Claus Westermann addressed the neglected topic of the collection of the psalms into the Hebrew Psalter.[1] In that brief study, he noted that nearly all of the psalms in the initial Davidic collection of Pss 3–41 are songs of the individual and that the individual lament category is predominant in that collection.[2] Westermann's brief analysis brought him to several conclusions, the first two being the most important for our purposes: "At first glance we can see that the lament of the individual, the most abundant category in the Psalter, is almost totally concentrated in the first half, and that means, of course, in the two large collections, Pss 3–41 and 51–72."[3] His second conclusion is that "larger groups of Psalms of praise appear *only* in the second half of the Psalter . . . The resultant picture is quite clear: The first half of the Psalter is composed predominantly of Psalms of lament, the second predominantly of Psalms of praise."[4] This last sentence, at least in English-language studies, has taken on the air of orthodoxy in Psalms scholarship. I put it this way: "The dominant psalm type in the first part of the Psalter is lament, and especially individual lament. The Psalter moves toward praise and the involvement of the entire community. Thus the organization of the book reflects the movement in the life of faith from death to life."[5]

In the Anglo-American world, the works of Brevard Childs on canon gave considerable impetus to the study of the shape and shaping of the Psalter.[6] The work that brought these matters to the fore in Psalms study is the published dissertation of Childs' student Gerald Wilson.[7] Gerald grew up in Waco, Texas, and completed his undergraduate studies at Baylor University prior to attending Fuller Theological Seminary and Yale University. Wilson's work is a redactional study. He reviews collections of psalms in the ancient Near East and reviews the markers in the Hebrew Psalter that suggest an intentional collection of the collections of psalms and of separate psalms. He concludes that Books I–III have a different editorial history than Books IV–V. The first three books reflect the experience of the Davidic kingdom, beginning with the coronation of the Davidic king in Ps 2 and reaching a conclusion with the fall of Jerusalem at the end of Ps 89. Books IV–V respond to the crisis of exile initiated by this defeat with a reassertion of the kingship of YHWH as the basis of the community's future. Some have questioned this macrostructure for the Hebrew Psalter because of Davidic elements in Books IV–V and because of the presence of lament in these latter parts of the Psalter, but Wilson's articulation of the reign of YHWH as central to the Hebrew

Psalter has had considerable influence in American scholarship.[8] Wilson's study of the Hebrew Psalter's redaction has in many readings of the Psalter been combined with Westermann's form-critical and redactional reading to solidify the psalmic movement from individual lament to community praise as central to the Psalms. Wilson's proposal provides a plotline for readers to follow as they make their way through the canonical Hebrew Psalter, and I think that accounts for a good portion of the proposal's popularity.

This movement mirrors what has been, in the tradition of Hermann Gunkel, the movement of the lament psalm itself. The standard articulation of the genre is that it addresses YHWH with a crisis, petitions for divine aid, and in a variety of fashions then undergoes the sudden change of mood to an expression of *die Gewissheit der Erhörung* (the certainty of a hearing) by way of a statement of certainty or trust or praise. Westermann's articulation of this movement of the lament genre has been very influential in Anglo-American scholarship and has been popularized in the works of Walter Brueggemann.[9] It seems to me that the established form-critical tradition has been strongly influenced by that articulation of the lament genre, and it has greatly influenced how many scholars have come to read the Psalter as a whole. Books I–III reflect the experience of lament, which then transitions to praise of the community with the turn to the Enthronement Psalms in Book IV and continues to the fivefold doxological conclusion of the Psalter. McCann suggests that the transition begins in Book III.[10] It also appears to me that what happens with both the Gunkel/Westermann definition of the lament genre and the corresponding definition of the shape of the Hebrew Psalter is that lament is diminished in these interpretive schemes. Lament becomes a prelude to praise or the first act in a drama whose goal is praise. At least in American culture, the neglect of lament fits the cultural norms of denying death and pain. As a result, many readers miss some of the anguished depths of these texts; I find that cultural bias to be present in both liturgy and scholarship.

What has happened in recent decades is something of a redefinition of the lament genre. Frederico Villanueva's cleverly titled study *The 'Uncertainty of a Hearing'* has made it clear that we have made too much of the sudden change of mood in lament psalms.[11] Lament psalms often conclude at a different place for the lamenter than they began, but the change is often not sudden and indeed the change may be from trouble to hope and back to trouble. Psalm 12, a lament with both individual and community dimensions, pleads for help in crisis and comes to a word of hope from YHWH in v. 6, characterized in the next verse as pure divine promises:

"Because the poor are despoiled, because the needy groan,
  I will now rise up," says the LORD;
"I will place them in the safety for which they long."
  The promises of the Lord are promises that are pure,
  silver refined in a furnace on the ground, purified seven times. (vv. 5-6)

The psalm ends with the clear and troubling presence of the wicked and of evil.

On every side the wicked prowl,
  as vileness is exalted among humankind. (v. 8)

A number of laments conclude with petition for help (e.g., Pss 25; 28). Those of us who have been educated as form critics tend to look for the typical rather than the distinctive in these poems. As a result, we have said that the lament genre is sufficiently flexible that we find ways to discount the exceptions to our prescriptive view that laments end positively. In addition, Uwe Rechberger's volume has made it crystal clear that the influential priestly salvation oracle hypothesis proposed by Begrich as the explanation of the sudden change of mood in the laments is no longer sustainable.[12] And we are now pleased to have in English Bernd Janowski's *Arguing with God*.[13] His study defines the lament genre in terms of a continuing spectrum, moving between trouble and trust, and shows that while lament psalms often move from greater trouble to greater trust, trust was never completely absent. If it were, the strong presence of the lament genre in the cult would be difficult to explain. So, in my view, we have seen a redefinition of the lament genre in Psalms studies; now we need to mirror that development in the explorations of the shape of the Psalter as a whole. To put the question in a stark way: if the book of Psalms moves from individual lament to community praise, why are the parade examples of imprecatory psalms (Pss 109; 137)—not to speak of other laments—in Book V of the Psalter? That is a question an undergraduate student asked in my class. I answered like a form critic answering a question about distinctive expressions of the lament genre: Well, there is some flexibility, but the broad movement, the typical change, is from lament to praise. Another part of the changed context in which we work is what has come to be called the new form criticism. Hermann Gunkel was a brilliant reader of texts, and he shaped the discipline of form criticism. He saw the connection between the language of psalms and the community life settings of their origin as well as their theological content. More recent scholars such as Martin Buss seek to reformulate the form criticism of Gunkel's work for contemporary scholarship. Buss defines form criticism as practices that simultaneously attend to human life processes, thoughts and feelings, and language.[14] So for Buss, language,

content, and *Sitz im Leben* are included in questions of genre in particular
social settings. These various dimensions of genre relate to each other not
rigidly but also not arbitrarily. Gunkel emphasized the typical; a number of
recent interpreters have emphasized the distinct artistic poetry of texts. Harry
Nasuti's volume on genre in Psalms interpretation emphasizes the continuing
importance of form criticism for Psalms interpretation, and suggests that the
reception history of these texts may also provide some helpful clues.[15] The
question of genre continues to be central to Psalms interpretation; what has
changed is the context in which we operate as interpreters. Form-critical
conclusions are held more tentatively, and the lines between categories are
no longer solid lines but are dotted lines. Ancient psalmists did not have some
rigid ancient Near Eastern template to follow. Questions of genre are in the
end reader- and hearer-generated issues. Genres serve to confirm or modify
interpreter expectations in the process of articulating meaning. I think there
is more here, and that has brought me to the relationship of praise and lament
in the latter parts of the Psalter.

A Matter of Poetics

Methodology

I need to say something further about methodology as I move forward. I
have been educated as a form critic and think that task is essential in Psalms
study. We practice that art, however, in a time when forms or genre are more
descriptive than prescriptive in the interpretive task and in a context in which
our conclusions must be held more tentatively than dogmatically. I have
suggested elsewhere that we consider again Westermann's basic impulse that
songs of plea and praise constitute the forms of the Psalms and that the lines
between even these genres need to be dotted lines rather than solid lines.[16]

As I have already indicated, I am in this chapter combining the form-
critical perspective with what in the American context often carries the label
of "the shape and shaping of the Psalter." I tend to settle on the shape side
of that compromise equation. I have no doubt that the Hebrew Psalter was
edited, and I understand the exploration of that process to be vital to the
scholarly task. I also believe that an articulation of much of that process
is lost in the erosion of time. What I am more interested in is the shape of
the Hebrew Psalter, in this final chapter on Books IV and V. How informed
readers or hearers interpret these texts to produce meaning is the task at hand.
Now please understand that I am not suggesting an ahistorical reading of the

Psalms. I attend to cultural codes that reflect these texts' sociohistorical origin, and I suggest that Books IV and V reflect the crisis of exile and its aftermath. Indeed, I come more and more to think that the Psalter as a whole deals with theodicy issues forged by the experience and aftermath of exile. I am, however, very cautious about such historical-critical matters. I find myself more on the synchronic side of the equation than the diachronic side. Attempting to make sense of the literary shape of Book V provides for me a constructive interpretive ground. In this literary-critical work, I have found the approach of poetics to be helpful. Poetics is "the systematic study of texts as literature, attending to artistic aspects and how they impact readers."[17] I have already noted the primacy effect. The beginnings and endings of texts, the sequences they follow, their points of view, characterizations, and connections to other texts provide significant interpretive clues to readers. By way of retrospective patterning, readers or singers draw interpretive conclusions about psalms.

By extension, I find the approach of poetics applicable to the shape of the Psalter. Readers begin with the introductory Pss 1 and 2 and make their way through the various collections of psalms in a reading process with various twists and turns along the way. Westermann is correct that most of the psalms in Book I reflect the trouble of being gripped by powers of death and evil. Readers of Book II will be pressed by the unrelenting power and presence of persistent enemies, though an emphasis on refuge in YHWH is also present in Books I–II. A variety of perspectives is characteristic of anthologies such as the Psalter. Book III moves more explicitly to the fall of Jerusalem (Pss 74; 79; 89) and the crisis that defeat brings. The conclusion of Book III, with the unrelenting lament of Ps 88 and the powerful articulation of the significance of the fall of the kingdom in Ps 89, leaves perceptive readers in a difficult place. And so my question is where the journey with praise and lament takes the interpretive community in the latter parts of the Hebrew Psalter. Book IV begins with a prayer of Moses (Ps 90) and so takes the community back to the time before the Davidic kingdom and very quickly moves to the power-ful celebration of the reign of YHWH (Pss 93–100). Community psalms of praise are strongly present in these latter parts of the Psalter. Book V also reflects the setting of exile and its aftermath. Psalm 119 with its emphasis on YHWH's Torah brings an imposing presence and is followed by the collection of pilgrimage songs (Pss 120–134) portraying a community yearning for the divine presence. An additional collection of Davidic psalms (Pss 138–145) reasserts the importance of lament and moves to the fivefold doxological conclusion of the Psalter.

Boris Uspensky suggests that the beginnings and endings of texts serve as a frame.[18] Readers move into the frame and the world of the text. Beginnings, Pss 1–2 and Book I of the Psalter, create the first impression of the framed text and strongly influence the expectations of readers. These first impressions, the primacy effect, tend to last as long as the textual data will allow.[19] From the formative beginnings, the reading process will move forward and take various paths, always in conversation with first impressions. The dominant presence of lament in Book I of the Psalter will continue to influence readers of the Hebrew Psalter. The ordering of the psalms is thus essential in the art of interpretation. I would suggest that there is a kind of arc from the beginnings of the Hebrew Psalter to its endings; that frame is essential for reading the book as a whole. So the extensive Book V and its conclusion are formative for the retrospective patterning readers perform in their interpretive work.

Egbert Ballhorn has provided us with a major contribution on the import of the conclusion of the Psalter.[20] If I have understood Ballhorn aright (always a serious question), he will agree with much of my approach so far. He argues that the order of the psalms makes a statement and is one of the book's structural features that communicates with readers. He bolsters Westermann's assertion that the Psalter moves from lament to praise. Ballhorn and I agree that the shape of the Psalter provides readers with signals recommending interpretive directions and goals. By *readers* he means readers implied by the text with its interpretive direction.[21] His work argues that the last word in the overall presentation gets the greatest weight and so dominates the interpretation. The different kind of doxology at the conclusion of Book V, after the scheme of all the other book-concluding doxologies, is a signal of the highest importance because it makes clear that the Psalter as a whole does not conclude in the same way that the first four books conclude.[22] Ballhorn argues that the Psalter has a limited narrative structure, with individual psalms that move from lament to praise, and ends as a book of praises.[23] Ballhorn's view is that the conclusion of the Psalter is literally and hermeneutically its last word in shaping the context for reading the individual psalms. Various themes emerge in Books IV–V, but the conclusion of the Psalter puts those themes in context. The Psalter is a kind of anthology with a conclusion that directs readers. I will return to Ballhorn's work later, but let me conclude this section by saying that his volume is a vigorous assertion of the hermeneutical importance of the conclusion of the Psalter. There is much to commend the approach, and I agree that the conclusion of the Psalter is formative for our reading. My qualification goes back to the significance of the primacy effect. That is, I would suggest that it is the conclusion of the Psalter in dialogue with the beginning of the Psalter that frames our reading. I agree that the last two books have a different accent than the first three,[24] and it is that difference in accent that I now want to explore further in five perspectives. The accents of the grammar are important clues for singers and readers/hearers of these texts. Each perspective suggests that lament/protest persists in Books IV–V as part of the larger life of faith characterized by both praise and lament.

AN EXPLORATION OF DIRECTIONS
IN THE PSALTER AS GRAMMAR OF FAITH

The Reign of YHWH

First, I want to return to Gerald Wilson's proposal centered on the assertion of the reign of YHWH in Book IV. I have already suggested that the initiation of Book IV with a Mosaic psalm suggests a move back to a time prior to the Davidic kingdom, which has fallen at the end of Ps 89. Book IV moves quickly to a sustained affirmation of divine rule in Pss 93–100, and Wilson understands the affirmation as a response to the fall of the Davidic kingdom portrayed at the end of Book III. Book IV opens with the Mosaic prayer as a community lament, reflecting the crisis of exile; that theme continues in Pss 90–92 and includes the hope of divine refuge. Psalms 93–100 press the theme to that of the reign of YHWH. Psalm 93 announces the theme, and the succeeding psalms celebrate various dimensions of it. The community is called to sing a new song, for hope and justice and faithfulness are possible in the kingdom of YHWH. These psalms provide a hopeful response to the crisis of exile. Psalms 102–106 call the community to come to terms with the crisis of exile in the context of the reign of YHWH. The reign of YHWH is the central theme of Book IV, but it is placed squarely in the context of the trauma of exile. The progression of the psalms makes that point.

Book IV calls the community to return to a setting prior to the Davidic monarchy, the time of Moses, as indicated in the book's opening psalm of Moses (Ps 90). In the wilderness time, the community encountered sovereign YHWH's persistent love and fidelity. The hope is that the community can experience that again in the wilderness of exile after the fall of the Davidic kingdom and live into the reign of YHWH as a way forward in this time of defeat and exile and chaos. The placement of the affirmation of the rule of YHWH in the midst of exile is central to Book IV of the Psalter and to the Psalter as a whole. Questions of theodicy must now include the confession of faith that YHWH reigns. Psalm 102 also provides a clear example. Verse 12 affirms the enthronement of YHWH:

> But you, YHWH, sit enthroned forever
> and memory of you continues generation after generation. (my translation)

At the same time, the text portrays the rubble in which Zion takes its current form in the verses that follow. The psalm integrates the affirmation of divine rule in the context of the community's trouble and woe.

> You will arrive and have compassion on Zion,
> for it is time to be gracious to her;
> for the appointed time has come.
> For your servants hold her stones dear,
> and her rubble they pity.
> Then nations will fear the name of YHWH
> and all the kings of the earth your glory,
> for YHWH will rebuild Zion
> and appear in glory
> and turn to the prayer of the forsaken
> and not despise their prayer. (vv. 13-17, my translation)

The poem's concluding section continues to seek to integrate faith in the reign of YHWH and the reality of exile. The confession of faith is in dialogue with the community's trouble. The confession of faith is that YHWH reigns even in the wilderness setting of exile. The confession of faith is more than a report of tradition. The poetry seeks to create in the community's imagination the hope and reality for living in the reign of YHWH. The theme of the assertion of divine rule in the midst of the suffering of exile and its aftermath continues in Book V. Note the conclusion of Book IV—

> Save us, O LORD our God,
> and gather us from among the nations. (Ps 106:47)

—and the beginning of Book V in Psalm 107:1-3 where God has gathered in the redeemed "from the lands," which suggests that the final book will relate to the aftermath of exile. Assertions of the reign of YHWH in Book V are even more closely tied to the community's suffering in the aftermath of exile. The hope is that the persistent love and fidelity of YHWH will come to reality in the current trouble and woe. The opening psalm of Book V narrates memories of how the community in the past encountered divine *ḥesed*. The conclusion of the Psalter emphasizes the reign of YHWH as a way into the future. The poetic celebrations of the reign of God in Book IV make it possible for the reading and praying community to imagine life in the reign of God and so to live it, even in the face of trouble and woe.

I take that assertion of divine kingship as an approach to questions of theodicy to be in line with a number of approaches in Christian theology.[25] McCann's understanding of the Psalter's affirmation of the reign of YHWH as both present and opposed, along with his eschatological reading of the Psalter, is one way to approach the subject. Other interpreters would emphasize the liturgical setting of the enthronement psalms in Book IV. Mowinckel famously understood liturgy as reality-generating drama with creative power.[26] The drama of the liturgy makes it possible for the congregation to imagine a social reality or a world to inhabit, a world in which YHWH reigns. The poetry seeks to draw the community into that reality. The interpretive community can imagine life in the reign of YHWH and live that life. As we saw in earlier chapters, poetry makes possible a new way of looking at the world and life. The drama of liturgical poetry can have a very persuasive effect.[27]

The Tradition of Protest

So one of the approaches to issues of theodicy centers on the affirmation of divine rule especially articulated in Book IV, though present in various parts of the Psalter. Anthologies, however, are not limited to a single approach. A second approach also pervades the Psalter and could be labeled the tradition of protest exhibited in Book V. The tradition goes back earlier in the Psalter. I have already noted the laments over the fall of Jerusalem in Pss 74; 79; 89 in Book III. The Korahite psalms continue the tone of lament and the need for hope in Zion. The loss of the community's center in Jerusalem and its temple colors much of Book III. Psalm 44 of Book II—a Korahite psalm— may also relate to that crisis. These prayers to YHWH are alarmingly honest; they detail the anguish of the community. I have called these prayers protest literature. Robert Cole notes the persistent questions of "Why?" and "How long?" in these psalms.[28] The questions of suffering here do not take the shape of theoretical issues of theology but of the honest dialogue between the faith community and YHWH. The overpowering crisis of exile is at the fore; chaos is not only knocking at the door but also flooding through the gate.

Book III, Pss 73–89, has been central to proposals for the shape of the Hebrew Psalter. Wilson's influential proposal suggests that after the introductory Ps 1, Ps 2 initiates the Davidic kingdom with a royal psalm related to the coronation.[29] The Davidic kingdom comes to an end with the fall of Jerusalem narrated in Ps 89, the conclusion of Book III. Books IV and V reply to the crisis of that defeat and the ensuing wilderness of exile. McCann suggests that the transition had already begun in Book III.[30] My study of Book III lends support to McCann's view and suggests even more strongly that the crisis of exile is very much present in Pss 73–89.

Book III begins with the Asaphite collection (Pss 73–83). This collection begins with an individual lament worrying over the prosperity of the wicked and moves to a community lament anguished over the destruction of the Jerusalem temple. The loss of this center for living pervades much of Book III. The destruction of the temple and of Jerusalem was catastrophic for this people, but the Psalms of Asaph continue to confess the sovereignty of YHWH. The praying community now awaits the demonstration of that sovereignty and in the meantime remembers the mighty acts of God. Psalm 79 also portrays the devastating destruction of the beautiful city of Zion/Jerusalem; the plight of this community of faith is heartbreaking.

> O God, the nations have come into your inheritance;
> they have defiled your holy temple;
> they have laid Jerusalem in ruins. (v. 1)

The Psalms of Asaph speak in very candid ways the community's pleas for justice. At the same time, Ps 80 in this collection includes a prophetic call for faithfulness on the part of the people.

The Korahite collection follows in Pss 84–85 and 87–88, and continues with lament and yearning for hope in YHWH's presence in Zion. Psalm 86 is an individual lament. The final two psalms of Book III press upon YHWH the pressing needs of the individual of faith and of the community of faith. Psalm 88 is one of the most anguished prayers in all of Scripture; Ps 89 concludes the book with the fall of the Davidic kingdom. Book IV responds to this crisis of defeat and exile.

In Book III, the protest continues in the context of faith. The crisis of chaos and defeat pervades the book. Enemies persist as the community's opposition, but the focus of the book is the raw and honest dialogue of faith between the community and YHWH. The prayers are brutally honest. I have dubbed them protest literature; the defeat and trouble of the community and its people of faith are at the fore. I have noted the use of "Why?" and "How long?" From its beginning (Ps 73), Book III has centered on questions of theodicy. It is the problem of defeat and exile that has brought such questions to the fore. In this context, theodicy is not a theoretical theological matter.

> It takes the shape of protest poems brought into the honest dialogue of faith.
> So while enemies are present, the focus is the dialogue between the faith

community and YHWH. These psalms thus instruct in prayer by example and envision a worship community that persistently and honestly presses the raw issues of life in the relationship with the divine.[31]

The world envisioned in Book III is enmeshed in a world filled with chaos and defeat; in that crisis the honest dialogue of faith persists. The task presented to the community of faith is to continue to live with these questions and claim them as part of faith.

The theme continues in Book IV with Pss 90; 94; 102; and 106. Book V intensifies the dialogue with the imprecatory Pss 109 and 137, harrowing protests against evil and evil ones. Psalm 109 is a blatant cry for divine vengeance in the face of false accusation. Psalm 137 is the infamous and raw cry of grief over the fall of Jerusalem and the cry for divine vengeance against those who have destroyed the community. Psalm 140 continues this theme of the search for divine justice; Pss 141–143 exhibit related calls for justice to rain down upon evil opponents. These texts focus on protest aimed at the divine rather than on theological articulations in the face of theodical questions all too familiar in life eked out in the context of exile and its aftermath.[32] The pervasive laments in Books I and II anticipate the issues around exile and theodicy; protest persists in all of the Hebrew Psalter.

I first came to this articulation of the issue some time ago in reading and reviewing *Defending God: Biblical Responses to the Problem of Evil* by James Crenshaw.[33] I found the volume to be helpful but was struck by how little it attended to the tradition of protest literature. Terrence Tilley's volume *The Evils of Theodicy* also steers away from traditional theological attempts to answer the questions of theodicy as theory that is not helpful to life and can actually thus support structures of evil.[34] The Psalter's dealing with theodical issues centers on protest and is in line with various dimensions of Jewish tradition.[35] The divine is held accountable, in line with post-Holocaust theology. The question of theodicy calls not for an answer but for a continuation and deepening of the tradition and practice of the protest of candor spoken to YHWH. Such an approach is embodied in the Hebrew Psalter and has influenced generations of those who read, hear, pray, and sing the Psalms.[36]

A "Spiritual Pilgrimage"

Third, Erich Zenger has produced one of the most interesting treatments of Book V. His conclusion is that Book V is "post-cultic and meant to be recited/meditated upon as a 'spiritual pilgrimage' to Zion, which is the seat of the universal king, YHWH, and of the God of Sinai who teaches his Torah from Zion."[37] This proposal fits with the view of Zenger and Hossfeld noted in chapter 4, which speaks of a postcultic setting for the book of Psalms as a whole with an emphasis on the encounter with the divine in the book itself. Book V is postcultic in the sense that it is a redactional composition. Zenger suggests that it fits the historical practice of reading the Psalms as a substitute for pilgrimage.[38] It is clearly the case that Torah is central in Book V. Psalm 119 has a dominating presence in the book as an extensive meditation on Torah. Zenger again:

> The acrostic Psalm 119 in the middle of the fifth book is a prayer for the grace to keep and love the Torah as the fundamental law of the announced and praised kingdom of God, so that the kingdom may come. In terms of the literary form it is an individual who is speaking here. But in terms of the compositional context, those praying are from Israel *and* the nations.[39]

While they do not use the term "Torah," Psalms 111–112 introduce the Egyptian Hallel with allusion to Torah in terms of the commandments and righteousness. King YHWH is certainly the righteous one who reveals life-giving Torah. Pilgrimage is also significant in the book with the Songs of Ascents as a collection tied to pilgrimage to Jerusalem/Zion. There is also a sense of the journey ancient Israel has taken with allusions to the exodus tradition in several psalms. My questions relate to the proposal of a postcultic setting. I agree that the book of Psalms is meant to be read and meditated upon, but I find it a false dichotomy to suggest that the Psalms are not also to be sung and heard. I understand the Psalter to be both prayer book and hymnbook. The psalms of praise in Book V do seem to be associated with liturgy.[40] I find that no less true of the lament elements in this fifth book. At the same time, I do not take these texts to be limited to liturgy. They also reveal wisdom and faith. As part of a grammar of faith, they both teach and sing. The variety of perspectives fits an anthology. The various collections of texts in Book V bear witness to the God who comes to deliver, is present to bless, and speaks to guide.

A Context for Book V

One of the recent volumes that contributes to our look at the latter parts of the Psalter is Dennis Tucker's *Constructing and Deconstructing Power in Psalms 107–150*.[41] The central claim of the study is that Book V of the Psalter asserts that the only reliable power for the ancient reading community of Book V is YHWH the creator. That claim requires a deconstructing of the ideology of the Achaemenid dynasty, which asserted that Ahuramazda, the god of earth and heaven, had placed all nations under Cyrus, Cambyses, and Darius. The empire's conquering "secures cosmic order" and thus "joyful participation by the conquered peoples."[42] The benefits of order come to the peoples. Book V of the Psalter asserts that YHWH is the God of heaven and casts the empire as an oppressive power subjugating the community in Yehud following the Babylonian exile. This community is hardly joyfully participating in the cosmic order brought by the empire. Tucker thus reads Book V in the context of the Persian Era. The enemies in Book V then become representatives of the empire. Here Tucker follows the scholarly tradition of Harris Birkeland (and Mowinckel) in identifying the enemies as foreign oppressors.[43]

The context of Book V is crucial for this identification of the enemies. Tucker characterizes the book's introductory psalm as "a didactic meditation on Israel's deliverance out of exile."[44] We will see that the enemy in this text is portrayed as "the hand of ṣar," that is the power (hand) of Israel's political and military enemies. Ṣar is an inherently political term and so rendering it as "distress," as a number of English translations do, is inadequate at best. The oppressive threat of the ṣar in the empire continues in the first collection of psalms in Book V. Psalm 109, commonly interpreted as an individual complaint and imprecatory psalm, takes on a secondary use of complaint about oppression of a powerless people. Psalm 110 speaks of divine victory over the threatening powers. The Hallel of Pss 111–118 speaks of empires and enemy nations of past and present in negative terms. The Songs of Ascents (Pss 120–134) portray the context of the community in terms of oppression from foreign powers. Psalms 135–137 also recount the oppression of foreign empires and nations. Especially in the imprecatory Ps 137, the power of empire does not bring the joyous participation in cosmic order by conquered people but rather brings weeping and extreme complaint. The final Davidic collection of psalms (Pss 138–145) continues to complain of enemies and evildoers against the petitioners. Tucker understands Pss 138 and 144 to contextualize a secondary use of these traditions in terms of the oppression of imperial power. The final Hallel concluding the Psalter continues the emphasis on the deconstruction of imperial power and hope in YHWH only.

This view of the enemies and evildoers in Book V is most helpful in giving a context for understanding their identity and function. The enemies are political enemies in the context of the Persian Empire. I am inclined to agree with this context for the redacted shape of Book V. The various themes of the collection are related to this context. I do not think the enemies and evildoers carry the same identity or function in every psalm in the fifth book, but I think Tucker, following Zenger,[45] has rightly identified the background setting. It is an important piece of the puzzle in exploring the grammar of faith the Psalter reveals.

Praise and Lament in Book V

I need now to come more specifically to Book V and explore the interplay of praise and lament in this portion of the grammar. Following Ps 106, Book V begins with the announcement of a hopeful theme of gathering the redeemed from exile.

> O give thanks to the LORD, for he is good;
> for his steadfast love endures forever.
> Let the redeemed of the LORD say so,
> those he redeemed from trouble
> and gathered in from the lands,
> from the east and from the west,
> from the north and from the south. (Ps 107:1-3)

Following this psalm of thanksgiving, Ps 108 combines parts of Pss 57 and 60 to craft a lament fitting for the experience of exile, perhaps reflected in v. 3, and reminding the community of divine, and not human, help.[46] Psalm 109 provides the parade example of an individual imprecatory psalm. The book's opening cluster of psalms articulates both the exilic community's need and the hope for divine *ḥesed*. Then, to review, Pss 111–118 constitute a collection of hallelujah psalms followed by the imposing reflection on Torah in Ps 119 and the collection of Psalms of Ascents in Pss 120–134. Psalms 135–137 are added and lead to the Davidic collection in Pss 138–145. The fivefold doxology of Pss 146–150 concludes the Hebrew Psalter. The length of Book V, along with the fact that it includes several collections, makes it challenging to draw definitive conclusions about the significance of the sequencing of the psalms, but I want to consider the interplay between praise and lament.

The call to thanksgiving that begins Book V in Ps 107 continues in Pss 111–112, suggesting that praise endures even in exile. Psalm 112 includes the presence of "evil tidings" and of enemies and evildoers. In Ps 113, the trio of the poor and needy and barren woman exemplify those in need of divine deliverance. The contrast is between human need and divine assistance. Psalm 115 emphasizes the divine "steadfast love and . . . faithfulness" in contrast to human power and to the emptiness of idols. McCann says that the psalm is "congruent with the apparent purpose of Book V to address the crisis of exile and its aftermath."[47] Psalm 116 bears witness to the experience of deliverance from life-threatening trouble and the possibility of praise and thanksgiving to God even in the midst of trouble and woe. Psalm 118 continues in this direction. Again McCann:

> Book V begins by establishing a post-exilic perspective and by commending consideration of God's steadfast love. Not coincidentally perhaps, Psalm 118 begins and ends with the same verse that opens Book V (Ps. 107:1), suggesting the possibility that Psalms 107–118 together offer a perspective from which to face the reality of continuing oppression: recollection of God's past activity as a basis for petition and grateful trust in God's future activity on behalf of the people.[48]

My point is that the praise dominating the first clusters of psalms in Book V is not unadulterated praise; the experience of lament and complaint still inform the life of faith. The extensive meditation that follows in Ps 119 also reflects the experience of lament.

Psalms 120–134 make up the collection of pilgrimage songs characterized in the superscriptions as Songs of Ascents and articulate the community's yearning for the divine presence. The collection includes domestic poetry and centers on the joy of divine blessing and assistance. The pilgrimage is a time of joy and anticipation and reaches a benedictory conclusion with the divine blessing from Zion. At the same time, the collection begins with lament and conflict and anxiety. Psalms 123; 126; and 130 voice the laments of the pilgrim community. The collection interweaves praise and lament in the context of the memory of pilgrimage to YHWH's blessing. Psalms 135–136 continue the praise of God in contrast to idols and human tyrants. Psalm 137 presents the parade example of a community imprecatory psalm. It deeply grieves the fall of Zion and then pronounces harrowing benediction on those who bring just vengeance on Zion's destroyers.[49]

The Davidic collection of Pss 138–145 begins with thanksgiving and praise and concludes with praise. Tucker makes clear that the laments powerfully articulate human powerlessness and the violence of the wicked. These psalms exhibit a number of verbal links and consistently and persistently tie the experience of lament to oppression by evildoers. I agree with Tucker that the literary shape of the collection puts lament in the context of the hope for divine deliverance and the affirmation of the reign of God.[50] What I want to add is that the praise that forms the frame of this collection is not devoid of the experience of lament in terms of trouble and woe and in terms of the oppression of the wicked (Pss 138:7; 139:19-24). Psalm 144 refers to the "new song" for the divine king (v. 9) but still knows the plea to

rescue me from the cruel sword,
and deliver me from the hand of aliens,
whose mouths speak lies,
and whose right hands are false. (v. 11)

Psalm 145 concludes the collection with a hymn of praise, though even here vv. 14 and 20 raise the specter of lament and oppression. The Davidic collection interweaves praise and lament; in these texts the lines between the form-critical categories are dotted lines rather than solid lines.

Psalms 146–150 bring the Hebrew Psalter to a conclusion. I agree with Ballhorn that this different form of conclusion signals to the interpretive community that the conclusion is not to Book V but to the whole Psalter.[51] I also wonder if Ps 145:21 could serve as the doxological word at the end of Book V and lead to the fivefold doxological conclusion of the Psalter.

My mouth will speak the praise of the Lord,
and all flesh will bless his holy name forever and ever.

Psalm 146 sings praise to the divine king, but note that the widow and orphan are still very present to be oppressed by the wicked. Psalm 147 affirms passionately that it is good to sing praise to the creator who reigns, but note that the outcast, brokenhearted, and downtrodden are still present to be cast down. Psalm 148 piles calls to praise one upon another. All of these hymns of praise express both skepticism about human power and hope for the reign of YHWH. Psalm 149 sings a new song of praise to King YHWH, but those singing the praise of God in their throats are portrayed with "two-edged swords in their hands, to execute vengeance on the nations" (vv. 6-7). The Psalter's climactic praise of King YHWH is also not unadulterated.[52] The distinction between praise and lament is somewhat porous even in the concluding fivefold doxology. The Psalter's grammar of faith is open, including both praise and lament. I have always wondered about the form of the final Ps 150. It constitutes a series of summonses to praise.[53] Two brief reasons for praise are articulated in v. 2: YHWH's "mighty deeds" and "surpassing" greatness, but the concluding psalm is dominated by more than a dozen calls to praise. What are we to make of that formal observation? Might I suggest that it is a signal to readers and hearers that the worshiping community is summoned to complete, if you will, the hymnbook of praise by offering praise and thanksgiving to the creator who rules, even in the midst of the aftermath of life-crushing defeat? The Psalter ends not so much in the praise of God as in the call to live praising God, even in a world with chaos knocking at the door. McCann would say that the eschatological rule of YHWH is present though resisted. I would prefer to say that Book V makes it possible for the reading community to imagine life in the reign of God and to lean into that reality even in the face of the chaos still lurking at the door.[54]

Book V as a collection of collections interweaves and interrelates praise and lament. It is common to say that lament moves to praise in the final shape of the Psalter, but I would suggest that is something of an oversimplification. The new "Hallelujah" to the creator who reigns is strikingly present in the conclusion of the Psalter, but it is more specifically a call to sing and live that hallelujah in the face of the chaos of the aftermath of exile, a chaos that is at best tamed but certainly not destroyed. The praise at the end of the Psalter is part of the larger life of faith that includes, even requires, lament. So I might say that the relationship between praise and lament in Book V reaches an uneasy poetic resolution. The movement is not so much lament *to* praise as it is lament *and* praise. That fits the anthological character of the Psalter, a collection of collections.

I began this look at both lament and praise at the end of the Psalter in a recent term when I was reading again with my doctoral students Hermann Gunkel's *Einleitung in die Psalmen* and noticed that near the end of the chapter on the hymns, Gunkel comes to the question of the relationship of hymns to other genres:

> The "complaint psalms" are far removed from the hymns in which the tone of the moaning and the entreaty is expressed loudly and, as a result, are differentiated from the sound of jubilation in the hymns as starkly as possible. Nevertheless, even these two opposites have sometime been attracted, leading to several borrowings.[55]

Even the great creator of the *Gattungen* recognizes the interaction between hymns and complaints. I am not particularly interested in his histories of the development of the various genres, but he suggests that a number of hymns in Book V reflect a diminished enthusiasm.[56]

CONCLUSION

This chapter is very much a preliminary metanarrative analysis that deserves much more textual exploration. May I summarize? I have suggested that several narrative impulses stream through the latter part of the Hebrew Psalter:

1   Wilson's proposal of the reign of YHWH as the response to the fall of Jerusalem portrayed in Ps 89 at the end of Book III. That theme is important in Books IV–V.

2 The tradition of continuing protest in the imprecatory psalms and laments of Book V. The texts do not respond to the crisis so much as they protest in the face of the chaos.

3 Zenger's view that the fifth book is to be recited and meditated on in place of an actual pilgrimage to Zion, the universal seat of YHWH who reigns and teaches Torah. The dominating place of Ps 119 in Book V certainly affirms Torah as central to the divine-human relationship.

4 Tucker's proposal that the setting for crafting Book V is discovered in its resistance to Persian ideology. The final book is crafted in a setting of the aftermath of defeat and chaos.

5 I have begun to explore the relationship of praise and lament in Book V. The two are enmeshed, and both are inherent in the grammar of faith which is the Psalter.

One of the advantages to Wilson's proposal on the shaping of the Hebrew Psalter is that it helps readers follow the plot of this poetic collection. I have suggested multiple plots. Might it be the case that the scribal communities in the Persian Era or Hellenistic Era conceived of a variety of readers and thus entertained various versions of plots? The communities certainly sang and heard and read and prayed a variety of songs, and readers continue to entertain various directions. The Psalter is a robust anthology.

I began by questioning Westermann's conclusion that the Psalter moves from individual lament to community praise, from death to life. I would affirm that individual laments dominate Books I–II. With Book III, the community raises its voice more clearly to protest the fall of Jerusalem with responses celebrating the reign of YHWH in Book IV. Community hymns of praise continue in Book V but so do strong laments. So while Westermann's conclusion has the ring of truth, it still bears considerable examination. Ballhorn notes that at the end of the Psalter, the community is still singing or at least invited to sing.[57] I would suggest that the conclusion brings us as readers and hearers back to the beginning to sing and reflect upon the Psalter as divine instruction in both lament and praise. Psalms often end with a call for the community to sing and pray again, and so does the Psalter as a whole. Such singing in a variety of keys makes possible the pilgrimage of both lament and praise. This sung grammar which is the book of Psalms articulates faith itself as relationship with God.

NOTES

CHAPTER 1: THE BOOK OF PSALMS

1   William L. Holladay, *The Psalms through Three Thousand Years: Prayerbook of a Cloud of Witnesses* (Minneapolis: Fortress, 1993); Susan E. Gillingham, *Psalms through the Centuries, Volume One*, Blackwell Bible Commentaries (Malden, Mass.: Blackwell, 2008); idem, *Psalms through the Centuries: A Reception History Commentary on Psalms 1–72, Volume Two*, Blackwell Bible Commentaries (Hoboken, N.J.: Wiley & Sons, 2018).

2   See Holladay, *Psalms through Three Thousand Years*, 95–112.

3   Gillingham, *Psalms through the Centuries*, 44.

4   Holladay, *Psalms through Three Thousand Years*, 149–50; Gillingham, *Psalms through the Centuries*, 82–83. In *The First Recension to Psalms 1–2*, line 32, Ibn Ezra opines, "Only the ancient poetry of the Hebrews can reveal that God is the one and only God."

5   Holladay, *Psalms through Three Thousand Years*, 139–46.

6   Gillingham, *Psalms through the Centuries*, 305–7.

7   Gillingham, *Psalms through the Centuries*, 288.

8   Gillingham, *Psalms through the Centuries*, 29. Athanasius, *The Life of Antony and the Letter to Marcellinus*, trans. Robert C. Gregg with a preface by William A. Clebsch, The Classics of Western Spirituality (New York: Paulist, 1980), 109, 111.

9   Augustine, *Confessions*, 9.4.17 (Watts, LCL).

10   Holladay, *Psalms through Three Thousand Years*, 178.

11   Gillingham, *Psalms through the Centuries*, 125–28.

12   Gillingham, *Psalms through the Centuries*, 102–3.

13   Holladay, *Psalms through Three Thousand Years*, 195.

14   Martin Luther, "Preface to the Psalter," in *Luther's Works*, ed. Helmut T. Lehmann, trans. Charles M. Jacobs, vol. 35 (Philadelphia: Muhlenberg, 1960), 253–57.

15   John Calvin, *Commentary on the Book of Psalms*, trans. James Anderson (Grand Rapids: Eerdmans, 1949), xxxvii.

16   Calvin, *Book of Psalms*, xliv.

17   Holladay, *Psalms through Three Thousand Years*, 198–99.

18   Translation from Charles Garside Jr., "Calvin's Theology of Music: 1536–1543," *Transactions of the American Philosophical Society* 69 (1979): 33.

19   Holladay, *Psalms through Three Thousand Years*, 198.

20   Holladay, *Psalms through Three Thousand Years*, 219–23, 273–76.

21   Dorothy Day, *The Long Loneliness* (New York: Harper & Row, 1952), 80–81.

22   Thomas Merton, *Praying the Psalms* (Collegeville, Minn.: Liturgical Press, 1956), 15.

23   Gillingham, *Psalms through the Centuries*, 291–95.

24   Dietrich Bonhoeffer, *Letters and Papers from Prison*, ed. Eberhard Bethge, enl. ed. (New York: Macmillan, 1972), 40, 415; C. S. Lewis' volume remains a popular treatment of the Psalms (*Reflections on the Psalms* [New York: Harcourt Brace, 1958]).

25   See Holladay, *Psalms through Three Thousand Years*, 359–71, for his account of the growth of the popularity of Ps 23.

26   Gillingham, *Psalms through the Centuries*, 143–45.

27   Note Walter Brueggemann's insightful articulation of why people of faith find the Psalms so compelling and at the same time find much of the Psalter so objectionable: our "love-hate relationship" with the counterworld the Psalms voice (*From Whom No Secrets Are Hid: Introducing the Psalms*, ed. Brent A. Strawn [Louisville: Westminster John Knox, 2014], 8–9).

28   Kathleen Norris, *The Cloister Walk* (New York: Riverside Books, 1996), 90–107.

29   Norris, *Cloister Walk*, 94, 96.

30   Kevin Adams, "Ancient Words in a New Light," *Faith & Leadership*, November 30, 2009, https://www.faithandleadership.com/ancient-words-new-light.

31   Ludwig Wittgenstein, *Philosophical Investigations*, 3rd ed., trans. G. E. M. Anscombe (New York: Macmillan, 1968), paragraphs 371–74.

32   Paul L. Holmer, *The Grammar of Faith* (San Francisco: Harper & Row, 1978).

33   Holmer, *Grammar of Faith*, 17–19.

34   Holmer, *Grammar of Faith*, 20–22, 26–30. In her novel *The Beautiful Mystery* (New York: Minotaur, 2012), Louise Penny characterizes the monks who sing Gregorian chant in this way: "'We would give up everything for the music. It's all that matters to us.' Then he smiled. 'Gregorian chants aren't

just music and they're not just prayer. They're both, together. The word of God sung in the voice of God. We'd give up our lives for that.'"

35 See Gerald Prince, *A Grammar of Stories: An Introduction* (The Hague: Mouton, 1973), 9–10, 15.

36 Michael G. Harvey, "Wittgenstein's Notion of 'Theology as Grammar,'" *RelS* 25 (1989): 103 (italics in original). Harvey explores philosophical issues in the notion of a grammar of faith. See also Richard H. Bell, "Theology as Grammar: Is God an Object of Understanding?" *RelS* 11 (1975): 307–17.

37 Andrew Moore, *Realism and Christian Faith: God, Grammar, and Meaning* (Cambridge: Cambridge University Press, 2003), 74–75.

38 Moore, *Realism and Christian Faith*, 118. Note Kathleen Norris' quote of Sebastian Moore that "God behaves in the psalms in ways he is not allowed to behave in systematic theology" (*Cloister Walk*, 91).

39 Molly T. Marshall, "Plowing the Soil of the Heart: The Psalter and Spirituality," *American Baptist Quarterly* 21 (2002): 506.

40 See Prince, *A Grammar of Stories*, 15.

41 Peter M. Candler Jr., *Theology, Rhetoric, Manuduction, or Reading Scripture Together on the Path to God* (Grand Rapids: Eerdmans, 2006), 45.

42 See W. H. Bellinger Jr., *Psalms: A Guide to Studying the Psalter*, 2nd ed. (Grand Rapids: Baker Academic, 2012).

43 Hermann Gunkel and Joachim Begrich, *An Introduction to the Psalms: The Genres of the Religious Lyric of Israel*, trans. James D. Nogalski (Macon, Ga.: Mercer University Press, 1998; German Original 1933).

44 Sigmund Mowinckel, *The Psalms in Israel's Worship*, 2 vols. (New York: Abingdon, 1962).

45 Such a characterization of David suggests the relevance of such psalms to others who face crises. See Denise Dombkowski Hopkins, *Psalms: Books 2–3*, Wisdom Commentary (Collegeville, Minn.: Liturgical Press, 2016) for an exploration of women's voices in relation to such psalms.

46 See Bellinger, *Psalms: A Guide*, 10–11, for a full listing.

47 Walter Brueggemann, *The Message of the Psalms: A Theological Commentary* Augsburg Old Testament Studies (Minneapolis: Augsburg, 1984), 19–23 passim. Cf. Brueggemann, "Psalms and the Life of Faith: A Suggested Typology of Function," *JSOT* 17 (1980): 3–32; repr. in *The Psalms of the Life of Faith*, ed. Patrick D. Miller (Minneapolis: Fortress, 1995), 3–32; also idem, "Bounded by Obedience and Praise," *JSOT* 16 (1991): 63–92.

48 Gerald Henry Wilson, *The Editing of the Hebrew Psalter*, SBLDS 76 (Chico, Calif.: Scholars Press, 1985).

49 For more on Wilson's work, see chapter 5 below.

50 Cf. J. Clinton McCann Jr. ed., *The Shape and Shaping of the Psalter*, JSOT-Sup 159 (Sheffield, U.K.: JSOT Press, 1993); Nancy L. deClaissé-Walford, *Reading from the Beginning: The Shaping of the Hebrew Psalter* (Macon, Ga.:

Mercer University Press, 1997); Nancy L. deClaissé-Walford, ed., *The Shape and Shaping of the Book of Psalms: The Current State of Scholarship*, AIL 20 (Atlanta: Society of Biblical Literature, 2014).

51 Jerome F. D. Creach, *The Destiny of the Righteous in the Psalms* (St. Louis: Chalice, 2008). See also Brueggemann's proposal noted above.

52 See, for example, David C. Mitchell, *The Message of the Psalter: An Eschatological Programme in the Book of Psalms*, JSOTSup 252 (Sheffield, U.K.: Sheffield Academic, 1997); Jamie A. Grant, *The King as Exemplar: The Function of Deuteronomy's Kingship Law in the Shaping of the Book of Psalms*, AcBib 17 (Atlanta: Society of Biblical Literature, 2004).

53 Michael K. Snearly, *The Return of the King: Messianic Expectation in Book V of the Psalter*, LHBOTS 624 (New York: T&T Clark, 2016), 1.

54 William P. Brown, *Seeing the Psalms: A Theology of Metaphor* (Louisville: Westminster John Knox, 2002). For a recent treatment of Hebrew poetry, see F. W. Dobbs-Allsopp, *On Biblical Poetry* (Oxford: Oxford University Press, 2015).

55 Brown, *Seeing the Psalms*, 78. Brown also makes careful use of ancient Near Eastern iconography.

56 Brown, *Seeing the Psalms*, 215.

57 Norris provides a good example (*Cloister Walk*, 90–107); on the power of the poetic language of the Psalms, see *Cloister Walk*, 154–58.

58 Richard J. Clifford, *Psalms 1–72*, AOTC (Nashville: Abingdon, 2002), 60–61.

59 Bellinger, *Psalms: A Guide*, 67. Note Jacobson's comment that Ps 6 can be taken as a typical lament, a prayer formula (Nancy deClaissé-Walford, Rolf A. Jacobson, and Beth LaNeel Tanner, *Psalms*, NICOT [Grand Rapids: Eerdmans, 2014], 101–2).

60 DeClaissé-Walford, Jacobson, and Tanner, *Psalms*, 103, 106–7. Note the comments on the tradition of the church's identification of Ps 6 as a penitential psalm (101). J. Clinton McCann Jr. also notes, "On the one hand, God is responsible for the psalmist's plight; on the other hand, God is the psalmist's only hope" ("The Book of Psalms," *NIB* 4:705).

61 See Walter Brueggemann and William H. Bellinger Jr., *Psalms*, NCBC (Cambridge: Cambridge University Press, 2014), 50.

62 See Clifford's statement at the end of his treatment of the prayer, *Psalms 1–72*, 64. See also McCann, "The Book of Psalms," 4:705: "If all we can talk about in regard to sickness and suffering is viruses or germs, then we are in danger of removing God from the whole realm of the human experience of sickness, suffering, and death. Psalm 6 resists such a move."

63 DeClaissé-Walford, Jacobson, and Tanner, *Psalms*, 122–23.

64 Brueggemann and Bellinger, *Psalms*, 59.

65 Clifford, *Psalms 1–72*, 69–70.

66 McCann suggests that being created in the image of God implies suffering and that God is involved in that suffering. He compares the book of Job ("The Book of Psalms," 4:712–13).

CHAPTER 2: OUT OF THE DEPTHS

1   Aubrey R. Johnson, "The Psalms," in *The Old Testament and Modern Study: A Generation of Discovery and Research: Essays by the Members of the Society,* ed. H. H. Rowley (Oxford: Clarendon, 1951), 169.

2   Claus Westermann, *The Praise of God in the Psalms* (Richmond: John Knox, 1965); idem, *The Psalms: Structure, Content & Message,* trans. Ralph D. Gehrke (Minneapolis: Augsburg, 1980); idem, *Praise and Lament in the Psalms* (Atlanta: John Knox, 1981); idem, *The Living Psalms,* trans. J. R. Porter (Grand Rapids: Eerdmans, 1989).

3   Bernhard W. Anderson, *Out of the Depths: The Psalms Speak for Us Today,* 3rd ed. (Louisville: Westminster John Knox, 2000).

4   George Arthur Buttrick, *Psalms, Proverbs,* vol. 4, of *The Interpreter's Bible* (New York: Abingdon, 1955), 4.

5   Marshall, "'Plowing the Soil of the Heart," 500–504.

6   "תורה," *HALOT* 4:1711–12.

7   Brevard S. Childs, *Introduction to the Old Testament as Scripture* (Philadelphia: Fortress, 1979), 513.

8   In a preface to the 1542 Geneva Psalter, Calvin wrote: "Now what Saint Augustine says is true, that no one is able to sing things worthy of God unless he has received them from him. Wherefore, when we have looked thoroughly everywhere and searched high and low, we shall find no better songs nor more appropriate for the purpose than the Psalms. . . . And furthermore, when we sing them we are certain that God puts the words in our mouths, as if he himself were singing in us to exalt his glory." This quotation comes from Garside, "Calvin's Theology of Music," 33. This quotation is referenced and cited in chapter 1, n. 18.

9   For options to explain the change of mood, see W. H. Bellinger, *Psalmody and Prophecy,* JSOTSup 27 (Sheffield, U.K.: JSOT Press, 1984).

10 Joachim Begrich, "Das priesterliche Heilsorakel," *ZAW* 52 (1934): 81–92.

11 Erhard Gerstenberger, *Psalms: Part 1 with an Introduction to Cultic Poetry,* vol. 1, FOTL 14 (Grand Rapids: Eerdmans, 1988), 62.

12 Claus Westermann, "The Formation of the Psalter," in *Praise and Lament in the Psalms,* 257. For more on my discussion of Westermann's work, see chapter 5 below.

13 Here Elohim as part of the Elohistic Psalter.

14 Brueggemann and Bellinger, *Psalms,* 321.

15 Brueggemann and Bellinger, *Psalms,* 324.

16 Peter C. Craigie, *Psalms 1–50,* WBC 19 (Waco, Tex.: Word, 1983), 334.

17   Brueggemann and Bellinger, *Psalms*, 209.
18   Brueggemann and Bellinger, *Psalms*, 211.
19   David R. Blumenthal, *Facing the Abusing God: A Theology of Protest* (Louisville: Westminster John Knox, 1993), 107.
20   DeClaissé-Walford, Jacobson, and Tanner, *The Book of Psalms*, 415.
21   Marshall, "'Plowing the Soil of the Heart,'" 507.
22   John Goldingay, *Psalms. Volume 2: Psalms 42–89*, BCOTWP (Grand Rapids: Baker Academic, 2007), 658–59.
23   The text of the psalm is also problematic and so interpretation must be tentative.
24   DeClaissé-Walford, Jacobson, and Tanner, *The Book of Psalms*, 508–9.
25   Bellinger, *Psalmody and Prophecy*, 63–66.
26   Clifford, *Psalms 1–72*, 164.
27   DeClaissé-Walford, Jacobson, and Tanner, *The Book of Psalms*, 305.
28   Gerald T. Sheppard, "Theology and the Book of Psalms," *Int* 46 (1992): 145–47.
29   DeClaissé-Walford, Jacobson, and Tanner, *The Book of Psalms*, 479.
30   Clifford, *Psalms 1–72*, 264–65.
31   Goldingay, *Psalms. Volume 1: Psalms 1–41*, BCOTWP (Grand Rapids: Baker Academic, 2006), 163.
32   Goldingay, *Psalms 1–41*, 179–80.
33   Brueggemann and Bellinger, *Psalms*, 251.
34   DeClaissé-Walford, Jacobson, and Tanner, *The Book of Psalms*, 512.
35   Brueggemann and Bellinger, *Psalms*, 594; DeClaissé-Walford, Jacobson, and Tanner, *The Book of Psalms*, 979; John Goldingay, *Psalms. Volume 3: Psalms 90–150*, BCOTWP (Grand Rapids: Baker Academic, 2008), 669; Richard J. Clifford, *Psalms 73–150*, AOTC (Nashville: Abingdon, 2003), 293.
36   DeClaissé-Walford, Jacobson, and Tanner, *The Book of Psalms*, 118.
37   Carleen Mandolfo, *God in the Dock: Dialogic Tension in the Psalms of Lament*, JSOTSup 357 (Sheffield, U.K.: Sheffield Academic, 2002), 35–41.
38   Brueggemann and Bellinger, *Psalms*, 283.
39   William P. Brown, *Psalms*, IBT (Nashville: Abingdon, 2010), 140.
40   The psalm's superscription ties the prayer for forgiveness to David's taking of Bathsheba. I take that not to be a historical judgment but an important clue about the depth of the text and about a life context for reading the prayer. See Brueggemann and Bellinger, *Psalms*, 238; DeClaissé-Walford, Jacobson, and Tanner, *The Book of Psalms*, 453.
41   McCann, "The Book of Psalms," 806.
42   Note also that many "studies of silence that kills are by women" (Brueggemann and Bellinger, *Psalms*, 163).
43   Brueggemann and Bellinger, *Psalms*, 473–74.
44   Brueggemann and Bellinger, *Psalms*, 476.

45 Clifford, *Psalms 73–150*, 275.
46 Brueggemann and Bellinger, *Psalms*, 576. See Erich Zenger, *A God of Vengeance? Understanding the Psalms of Divine Wrath* (Louisville: Westminster John Knox, 1996).
47 Marshall, "'Plowing the Soil of the Heart,'" 501–2; Luther, "Preface to the Psalter."
48 Marshall, "'Plowing the Soil of the Heart,'" 502.
49 Walter Brueggemann, "The Costly Loss of Lament," *JSOT* 11 (1986): 57–71.
50 Marshall, "'Plowing the Soil of the Heart,'" 507.

CHAPTER 3: THE PRAISE OF GOD IN THE PSALMS

1 Westermann, *The Praise of God in the Psalms*; idem, *The Psalms*; idem, *Praise and Lament in the Psalms*; idem, *The Living Psalms*.
2 Hermann Gunkel, *The Psalms: A Form-Critical Introduction*, trans. Thomas M. Horner, Biblical Series 19 (Philadelphia: Fortress, 1967); Gunkel and Begrich, *Introduction to Psalms*.
3 DeClaissé-Walford, Jacobson, and Tanner, *Psalms*, 863.
4 McCann, "The Book of Psalms," 4:1150.
5 The superscription for Ps 30 suggests that it was used "at the dedication of the temple." Several commentators note the use of the psalm at Hanukkah and thus take this reference to be to the dedication of the temple after the desecration of Antiochus Epiphanes. Goldingay, *Psalms 1–42*, 425; DeClaissé-Walford, Jacobson, and Tanner, *Psalms*, 289–90; Clifford, *Psalms 1–72*, 157; McCann, "The Book of Psalms," 4:795. The scribal heading would then reflect continuing liturgical usage of an earlier psalm in the second century BCE.
6 DeClaissé-Walford, Jacobson, and Tanner, *Psalms*, 292–93; Goldingay, *Psalms 1–42*, 433.
7 Robert Alter, *The Art of Biblical Poetry*, new and rev. ed. (New York: Basic Books, 2011), 134–35; Goldingay, *Psalms 1–42*, 427–29.
8 See Bellinger, *Psalms: A Guide*, 84.
9 McCann, "The Book of Psalms," 4:1103.
10 Brueggemann and Bellinger, *Psalms*, 452. The phrase is from Martin Buber, *Moses: The Revelation and Covenant* (Atlantic Highlands, N.J.: Humanities Press International, 1988), 75.
11 DeClaissé-Walford, Jacobson, and Tanner, *Psalms*, 787.
12 McCann, "The Book of Psalms," 4:1104.
13 Brueggemann and Bellinger, *Psalms*, 416; Mowinckel, *Psalms in Israel's Worship*.
14 McCann, "The Book of Psalms," 4:1064–65.
15 James Luther Mays, *The Lord Reigns: A Theological Handbook to the Psalms*, IBC (Louisville: Westminster John Knox, 1994).

16   Hans-Joachim Kraus, *Psalms 60–150: A Commentary*, trans. Hilton C. Oswald (Minneapolis: Fortress, 1989), 254.

17   Annie Dillard, *Teaching a Stone to Talk* (New York: Harper & Row, 1982), 40–41.

18   Brueggemann and Bellinger, *Psalms*, 217.

19   Marshall, "Plowing the Soil of the Heart," 504. This quotation comes from Don Saliers, "Singing Our Lives," in *Practicing Our Faith: A Way of Life for a Searching People*, ed. Dorothy C. Bass (San Francisco: Jossey-Bass, 1997), 192.

20   Brueggemann and Bellinger, *Psalms*, 30–31.

21   George Wishart Anderson, "Israel's Creed: Sung, Not Signed," *SJT* 16 (1963): 277–85.

CHAPTER 4: THE SHAPE OF THE GRAMMAR

1   See W. H. Bellinger Jr., *A Hermeneutic of Curiosity and Readings of Psalm 61*, Studies in Old Testament Interpretation 1 (Macon, Ga.: Mercer University Press, 1995) for the eclectic approach I continue to espouse.

2   Childs, *Introduction to the Old Testament as Scripture*, 513–14.

3   Westermann, *Praise and Lament in the Psalms*, 250–58.

4   Wilson, *Editing of the Hebrew Psalter*.

5   David Willgren, *The Formation of the "Book" of Psalms: Reconsidering the Transmission and Canonization of Psalmody in Light of Material Culture and the Poetics of Anthologies*, FAT 2/88 (Tübingen: Mohr Siebeck, 2016), 1–9.

6   See McCann, "The Book of Psalms," 4:639–1280.

7   See Mays, *The Lord Reigns*; and deClaissé-Walford, *Reading from the Beginning*.

8   Mitchell, *Message of the Psalter*. See also Grant, *King as Exemplar*.

9   Snearly, *Return of the King*, 100–101.

10   Snearly, *Return of the King*, 187.

11   Snearly, *Return of the King*, 190.

12   Brueggemann, "Bounded by Obedience and Praise," 63–92.

13   Jerome F. D. Creach, *Yahweh as Refuge and the Editing of the Hebrew Psalter*, JSOTSup 217 (Sheffield, U.K.: Sheffield Academic, 1996); idem, *Destiny of the Righteous in the Psalms*.

14   Erich Zenger, "The Composition and Theology of the Fifth Book of Psalms, Psalms 107–145," *JSOT* 80 (1998): 77–102; idem, "Die Komposition der Wallfahrtpsalmen Ps 120–134: Zum Programm der Psalterexegese," in *Paradigmen auf dem Prüfstand: Exegese wider den Strich*, ed. Martin Ebner and Bernhard Heininger (Münster: Aschendorff, 2004), 173–90.

15   Frank-Lothar Hossfeld and Erich Zenger, *Die Psalmen I: Psalm 1–50*, NEchtB 29 (Würzburg: Echter Verlag, 1993); idem, *Psalms 2: A Commentary on Psalms 51–100*, trans. Linda M. Maloney, Hermeneia (Minneapolis: Fortress,

2005 [German original, 2000]); idem, *Psalms 3: A Commentary on Psalms 101–150*, trans. Linda M. Maloney, Hermeneia (Minneapolis: Fortress, 2011 [German original, 2008]).

16   Matthias Millard, *Die Komposition des Psalters: ein formgeschichtlicher Ansatz*, FAT 9 (Tübingen: J. C. B. Mohr, 1994).

17   David M. Howard, *The Structure of Psalms 93–100*, BJSUCSD 5 (Winona Lake, Ind.: Eisenbrauns, 1997).

18   R. Norman Whybray, *Reading the Psalms as a Book*, JSOTSup 222 (Sheffield, U.K.: Sheffield Academic, 1996).

19   Erhard Gerstenberger, "Der Psalter als Buch und als Sammlung," in *Neue Wege der Psalmenforschung*, ed. Klaus Seybold and Erich Zenger, Herders biblische Studien 1 (Freiburg: Herder, 1994), 3–13.

20   This account of scholarship has not attended to the Qumran materials. I have generally followed the view of Peter W. Flint, *The Dead Sea Psalms Scrolls and the Book of Psalms*, STDJ 17 (Leiden: Brill, 1997); idem, "The Book of Psalms in the Light of the Dead Sea Scrolls," *VT* 48 (1998): 453–72, though the nature of the Qumran materials is certainly debated. There have been various proposals for the date of the close of the Hebrew Psalter. I believe a case can be made for the view that the bulk of the Masoretic Psalter was in place around the time of the end of the Persian Period and the beginning of the Hellenistic Period. The faith community at that point would still be dealing with issues tied to the experience of exile.

21   See Shlomith Rimmon-Kenan, *Narrative Fiction: Contemporary Poetics* (London: Methuen, 1983).

22   Stanley Eugene Fish, *Is There a Text in This Class? The Authority of Interpretive Communities* (Cambridge: Harvard University Press, 1980).

23   See n. 5 above.

24   Willgren, *Formation of the "Book" of Psalms*, 24.

25   Willgren, *Formation of the "Book" of Psalms*, 116–32.

26   See Willgren, *Formation of the "Book" of Psalms*, 28–30.

27   Much more instructive scholarship will no doubt continue to surface with helpful constructions of ancient scribal practices and communities. At this point in time, however, I would point to Zenger's comments on the redaction of Book V of the Psalter. I may disagree with a number of his conclusions, but it seems to me that the overall brunt of his case suggests that at a minimum, the scribes who shaped the latter part of the Psalter were reading and sequencing the psalms together intentionally. See, for example, Zenger, "Composition and Theology," 77–102.

28   See Bellinger, *Hermeneutic of Curiosity*, 61.

29   Patrick D. Miller, "The Beginning of the Psalter," in *The Shape and Shaping of the Psalter*, ed. J. Clinton McCann Jr., JSOTSup 159 (Sheffield, U.K.: JSOT Press, 1993), 84–85.

30   J. Clinton McCann Jr., "Books I–III and the Editorial Purpose of the Hebrew Psalter," in *The Shape and Shaping of the Psalter*, ed. J. Clinton McCann Jr., JSOTSup 159 (Sheffield, U.K.: JSOT Press, 1993), 103–4.

31   Childs, *Introduction to the Old Testament*, 513.

32   Wilson, *Editing of the Hebrew Psalter*, 206.

33   Brueggemann, "Bounded by Obedience and Praise."

34   J. Clinton McCann Jr., *A Theological Introduction to the Book of Psalms: The Psalms as Torah* (Nashville: Abingdon, 1993), 43–45.

35   DeClaissé-Walford, *Reading from the Beginning*, 41–49; Mays also emphasizes both the reign of God and torah (*The Lord Reigns*).

36   Miller, "Beginning of the Psalter," 87.

37   Creach, *Yahweh as Refuge*, 80.

38   The delineation of clusters of psalms often begins with the collections referenced in superscriptions. Linguistic and thematic connections between psalms are also pertinent.

39   Brueggemann and Bellinger, *Psalms*, 58, 64.

40   Brown, *Seeing the Psalms*, 97–107.

41   W.H. Bellinger Jr., "Reading from the Beginning (Again): The Shape of Book I of the Psalter," in *Diachronic and Synchronic: Reading the Psalms in Real Time: Proceedings of the Baylor Symposium on the Book of Psalms*, ed. Joel S. Burnett, W.H. Bellinger Jr., and W. Dennis Tucker Jr., LHBOTS 488 (New York: T&T Clark, 2007), 114–26.

42   McCann, "The Book of Psalms," 4:660.

43   DeClaissé-Walford, Jacobson, and Tanner, *Psalms*, 396.

44   Brueggemann and Bellinger, *Psalms*, 304–5, 308.

45   Brueggemann and Bellinger, *Psalms*, 325.

46   Brueggemann and Bellinger, *Psalms*, 360.

47   Note Brown's comments about the Korahite collections and the place of Ps 88 in it (*Seeing the Psalms*, 93–94).

48   DeClaissé-Walford, Jacobson, and Tanner, *Psalms*, 581–83.

49   DeClaissé-Walford, Jacobson, and Tanner, *Psalms*, 583.

50   McCann, "The Book of Psalms," 4:1053.

51   Brueggemann and Bellinger, *Psalms*, 430–34.

52   Brown, *Seeing the Psalms*, 128.

53   Brueggemann and Bellinger, *Psalms*, 469–70.

54   Brueggemann and Bellinger, *Psalms*, 507.

55   DeClaissé-Walford, Jacobson, and Tanner, *Psalms*, 810.

56   See Brueggemann and Bellinger, *Psalms*, 573.

57   DeClaissé-Walford, Jacobson, and Tanner, *Psalms*, 811.

58   Susan Gillingham, "Psalmody and Apocalyptic in the Hebrew Bible: Common Vision, Shared Experience?," in *After the Exile: Essays in Honour of Rex Mason*, ed. John Barton and David J. Reimer (Macon, Ga.: Mercer

University Press, 1996), 147–69; Dennis Tucker Jr., "Empires and Enemies in Book V of the Psalter," in *The Composition of the Book of Psalms*, ed. Erich Zenger, BETL 238 (Leuven: Peeters, 2010), 723–31; Gerald Henry Wilson, "A First Century C.E. Date for the Closing of the Book of Psalms?" *JBQ* 28 (2000): 102–10.

59 W. H. Bellinger Jr., "The Psalter as Theodicy Writ Large," in *Jewish and Christian Approaches to the Psalms: Conflict and Convergence*, ed. Susan Gillingham (Oxford: Oxford University Press, 2013), 151–52.

60 McCann, "The Book of Psalms," 4:670.

61 Sigmund Mowinckel, *Psalmenstudien vol. 2: Das Thronbesteigungsfest Jahwäs und der Ursprung der Eschatologie* (Oslo: Jacob Dybwad, 1922). We now have an English version (Sigmund Mowinckel, "YHWH's Enthronement Festival and the Origin of Eschatology," in vol. 1 of *Psalm Studies*, trans. Mark E. Biddle, HBS 3 [Atlanta: Society of Biblical Literature, 2014], 173–491).

62 Robert L. Cole, *The Shape and Message of Book III (Psalms 73–89)*, JSOTSup 307 (Sheffield, U.K.: Sheffield Academic, 2000), 231–35.

CHAPTER 5: THE MOVEMENT OF THE GRAMMAR

1 Claus Westermann, "The Formation of the Psalter," in *Praise and Lament in the Psalms*, 250–58. First published as "Zur Sammlung des Psalters," *Theologia Viatorum* 8 (1962): 278–84.

2 Westermann, "Formation of the Psalter," 254.

3 Westermann, "Formation of the Psalter," 257.

4 Westermann, "Formation of the Psalter," 257.

5 Bellinger, *Psalms: A Guide*, 62.

6 See Childs, *Introduction to the Old Testament*, 504–25.

7 Wilson, *Editing of the Hebrew Psalter*. See also Martin Leuenberger, *Konzeptionen des Königtums Gottes im Psalter: Untersuchungen zu Komposition und Redaktion der theokratischen Bücher IV–V im Psalter*, ATANT (Zürich: Theologischer, 2004).

8 See Mays, *The Lord Reigns*; McCann, "The Book of Psalms"; deClaissé-Walford, *Reading from the Beginning*.

9 See, for example, Brueggemann, "The Costly Loss of Lament," in *The Psalms and the Life of Faith*, ed. Patrick D. Miller (Minneapolis: Fortress, 1995), 98–102.

10 McCann, "Books I–III," 93–107.

11 Frederico G. Villanueva, *The 'Uncertainty of a Hearing': A Study of the Sudden Change of Mood in the Psalms of Lament*, VTSup (Leiden: Brill, 2008).

12 Uwe Rechberger, *Von der Klage zum Lob: Studien zum "Stimmungsumschwung" in den Psalmen*, WMANT (Neukirchen-Vluyn, Germany: Neukirchener Verlagsgesellschaft, 2012).

13 Bernd Janowski, *Arguing with God: A Theological Anthropology of the Psalms*, trans. Armin Siedlecki (Louisville: Westminster John Knox, 2013).

14 Martin J. Buss, "Toward Form Criticism as an Explication of Human Life: Divine Speech as a Form of Self Transcendence," in *The Changing Face of Form Criticism*, ed. Marvin Sweeney and Ehud Ben Zvi (Grand Rapids: Eerdmans, 2003), 316.

15 Harry Nasuti, *Defining the Sacred Song: Genre, Tradition, and the Post-Critical Interpretation of the Psalms*, JSOTSup 218 (Sheffield, U.K.: Sheffield Academic, 1999).

16 See W. H. Bellinger, "Psalms and the Question of Genre," in *The Oxford Handbook of the Psalms*, ed. William P. Brown (Oxford: Oxford University Press, 2014), 313–25. We work in a context that values a plurality of interpretive possibilities. Even so, it seems to me that Westermann's basic impulse of the two literary types of psalms as praise and lament stands and fundamentally undergirds constructive readings of the Psalms.

17 See Bellinger, *Hermeneutic of Curiosity*, 89–107; idem, "Reading from the Beginning (Again)," 114–26. The quote is from 115.

18 Boris Uspensky, *A Poetics of Composition: The Structure of the Artistic Text and Typology of a Compositional Form*, trans. C. Zavarin and S. Wittig (Berkeley: University of California Press, 1973), 137, 149.

19 See Menakhem Perry, "Literary Dynamics: How the Order of a Text Creates its Meanings," *Poetics Today* 1 (1979): 35–64, 311–61; Mikeal C. Parsons, "Reading a Beginning/Beginning a Reading: Tracing Literary Theory on Narrative Openings," *Semeia* 52 (1990): 11–31; Edward W. Said, *Beginnings: Intention and Method* (New York: Basic Books, 1975); and Manfred Jahn, "Frames, Preferences, and the Reading of Third Person Narratives: Towards a Cognitive Narratology," *Poetics Today* 18 (1997): 441–68.

20 Egbert Ballhorn, *Zum Telos des Psalters: Der Textzusammenhang des Vierten und Fünften Psalmenbuches (Ps 90–150)*, BBB 138 (Berlin: Philo, 2004).

21 The text's communication model includes poets and scribes leading to a text received by audiences, hearers/readers who have interpreted the text in its earliest form and in successive generations.

22 Ballhorn, *Zum Telos des Psalters*, 50–51, 61.

23 Ballhorn, *Zum Telos des Psalters*, 30–31. Compare Robert Alter's suggestion that psalms have a narrative impulse: *Art of Biblical Poetry*, esp. 28.

24 Ballhorn, *Zum Telos des Psalters*, 373.

25 Compare Ballhorn, *Zum Telos des Psalters*, 382.

26 Mowinckel, *Psalms in Israel's Worship*, 2:21.

27 See Walter Brueggemann, *Israel's Praise: Doxology against Idolatry and Ideology* (Philadelphia: Fortress, 1988); and Bellinger, *Hermeneutic of Curiosity*, 21, 87, 110, 122.

28 Cole, *Shape and Message of Book III*, 231–35.

29 Wilson, *Editing of the Hebrew Psalter*, 209. See also deClaissé-Walford, *Reading from the Beginning*.
30 McCann, "Books I–III," 93–107.
31 Bellinger, "Psalter as Theodicy," 156.
32 See Terence W. Tilley, *The Evils of Theodicy* (Washington, D.C.: Georgetown University Press, 1991).
33 James L. Crenshaw, *Defending God: Biblical Responses to the Problem of Evil* (Oxford: Oxford University Press, 2005).
34 Tilley, *Evils of Theodicy*. See also Kenneth Surin, "Theodicy?" *HTR* 76 (1983): 225–47; Charles Pinches, "Christian Pacifism and Theodicy: The Free Will Defense in the Thought of John H. Yoder," *Modern Theology* 5 (1989): 239–55; David O'Connor, "In Defense of Theoretical Theodicy," *Modern Theology* 5 (1988): 61–74.
35 See Elie Wiesel, *The Trial of God* (New York: Schocken Books, 1979), vii.
36 Bellinger, "Psalter as Theodicy," 157–58.
37 Zenger, "Composition and Theology," 100.
38 Zenger, "Composition and Theology," 100.
39 Zenger, "Composition and Theology," 99.
40 Zenger, "Composition and Theology," 77–78, 99.
41 W. Dennis Tucker Jr., *Constructing and Deconstructing Power in Psalms 107–150*, AIL 19 (Atlanta: Society of Biblical Literature, 2014).
42 Tucker, *Constructing and Deconstructing Power*, 53.
43 Tucker, *Constructing and Deconstructing Power*, 12–15. I need to indicate that I find in Birkeland a kind of "patternism" in which a preconceived notion of enemies from community complaints is applied to individual complaints and the enemies there. I am more inclined to the separation of the portrayal of enemies and evildoers in community psalms and those in individual psalms.
44 Tucker, *Constructing and Deconstructing Power*, 59.
45 Erich Zenger, "Der jüdische Psalter—ein anti-imperiales Buch?," in *Religion und Gesellschaft: Studien zu ihrer Wechselbeziehung in den Kulturen des antiken Vorderen Orients*, ed. Rainer Albertz, AZERKAVO 1/AOAT 248 (Münster: Ugarit, 1997), 95–108.
46 Brueggemann and Bellinger, *Psalms*, 469–71.
47 McCann, "Book of Psalms," 4:1144.
48 McCann, "Book of Psalms," 4:1153–54.
49 See Brueggemann and Bellinger, *Psalms*, 573, on the connection of Ps 137 with its literary context.
50 See also Hossfeld and Zenger, *Psalms 3*, 6.
51 Ballhorn, *Zum Telos des Psalters*, 50–51, 61.
52 Hossfeld and Zenger, *Psalms 3*, 7, concur that the Psalter's fivefold doxology reflects both "the individual negative experiences of the world's reality" and

"the fundamental goodness of the world," though they read the conclusion of the Psalter with eschatological hope.

53 Hossfeld and Zenger, *Psalms 3*, 655.
54 Zenger notes that the praise at the end of the Book V is in a context of suffering ("Composition and Theology," 101).
55 Gunkel and Begrich, *Introduction to the Psalms*, 58.
56 Gunkel and Begrich, *Introduction to the Psalms*, 64.
57 Ballhorn, *Zum Telos des Psalters*, 368.

BIBLIOGRAPHY

Adams, Kevin. "Ancient Words in a New Light." *Faith & Leadership*, November 30, 2009. https://www.faithandleadership.com/ancient-words-new-light.

Alter, Robert. *The Art of Biblical Poetry*. New and rev. ed. New York: Basic Books, 2011.

Anderson, Bernhard W. *Out of the Depths: The Psalms Speak for Us Today*. 3rd ed. Louisville: Westminster John Knox, 2000.

Anderson, George Wishart. "Israel's Creed: Sung, Not Signed." *SJT* 16 (1963): 277–85.

Athanasius. *The Life of Antony and the Letter to Marcellinus*. Translated by Robert C. Gregg with a preface by William A. Clebsch. The Classics of Western Spirituality. New York: Paulist, 1980.

Augustine. *Confessions*. Translated by William Watts. 2 vols. LCL. Cambridge: Harvard University Press, 1977–1979.

Ballhorn, Egbert. *Zum Telos des Psalters: Der Textzusammenhang des vierten und fünften Psalmenbuches (Ps 90–150)*. BBB 138. Berlin: Philo, 2004.

Begrich, Joachim. "Das priesterliche Heilsorakel." *ZAW* 52 (1934): 81–92.

Bell, Richard H. "Theology as Grammar: Is God an Object of Understanding?" *RelS* 11 (1975): 307–17.

Bellinger, W. H., Jr. *A Hermeneutic of Curiosity and Readings of Psalm 61*. SOTI 1. Macon, Ga.: Mercer University Press, 1995.

———. *Psalmody and Prophecy*. JSOTSup 27. Sheffield, U.K.: JSOT Press, 1984.

———. *Psalms: A Guide to Studying the Psalter*. 2nd ed. Grand Rapids: Baker Academic, 2012.

———. "Psalms and the Question of Genre." In *The Oxford Handbook of the Psalms*, edited by William P. Brown, 313–25. Oxford: Oxford University Press, 2014.

———. "The Psalter as Theodicy Writ Large." In *Jewish and Christian Approaches to the Psalms: Conflict and Convergence*, edited by Susan Gillingham, 147–60. Oxford: Oxford University Press, 2013.

———. "Reading from the Beginning (Again): The Shape of Book I of the Psalter." In *Diachronic and Synchronic: Reading the Psalms in Real Time: Proceedings of the Baylor Symposium on the Book of Psalms*, edited by Joel S. Burnett, W. H. Bellinger Jr., and W. Dennis Tucker Jr., 114–26. LHBOTS 488. New York: T&T Clark, 2007.

Blumenthal, David R. *Facing the Abusing God: A Theology of Protest*. Louisville: Westminster John Knox, 1993.

Bonhoeffer, Dietrich. *Letters and Papers from Prison*. Edited by Eberhard Bethge. Enl. ed. New York: Macmillan, 1972.

Brown, William P. *Psalms*. IBT. Nashville: Abingdon, 2010.

———. *Seeing the Psalms: A Theology of Metaphor*. Louisville: Westminster John Knox, 2002.

Brueggemann, Walter. "Bounded by Obedience and Praise: The Psalms as Canon." *JSOT* 16 (1991): 63–92.

———. "The Costly Loss of Lament." *JSOT* 11 (1986): 57–71.

———. *From Whom No Secrets Are Hid: Introducing the Psalms*. Edited by Brent A. Strawn. Louisville: Westminster John Knox, 2014.

———. *Israel's Praise: Doxology against Idolatry and Ideology*. Philadelphia: Fortress, 1988.

———. *The Message of the Psalms: A Theological Commentary*. Augsburg Old Testament Studies. Minneapolis: Augsburg, 1984.

———. "Psalms and the Life of Faith: A Suggested Typology of Function." *JSOT* 17 (1980): 3–32. Repr. in *The Psalms of the Life of Faith*, edited by Patrick D. Miller, 3–32. Minneapolis: Fortress, 1995.

Brueggemann, Walter, and William H. Bellinger Jr. *Psalms*. NCBC. Cambridge: Cambridge University Press, 2014.

Buber, Martin. *Moses: The Revelation and Covenant*. Atlantic Highlands, N.J.: Humanities Press International, 1988.

Buss, Martin J. "Toward Form Criticism as an Explication of Human Life: Divine Speech as a Form of Self Transcendence." In *The Changing Face of Form Criticism*, edited by Marvin Sweeney and Ehud Ben Zvi, 312–25. Grand Rapids: Eerdmans, 2003.

Buttrick, George Arthur. *Psalms, Proverbs*. Vol. 4 of *The Interpreter's Bible*. New York: Abingdon, 1955.

Calvin, John. *Commentary on the Book of Psalms*. Translated by James Anderson. Grand Rapids: Eerdmans, 1949.

Candler, Peter M., Jr. *Theology, Rhetoric, Manuduction, or Reading Scripture Together on the Path to God*. Grand Rapids: Eerdmans, 2006.

Childs, Brevard S. *Introduction to the Old Testament as Scripture*. Philadelphia: Fortress, 1979.

Clifford, Richard J. *Psalms 1–72*. AOTC. Nashville: Abingdon, 2002.

———. *Psalms 73–150*. AOTC. Nashville: Abingdon, 2003.

Cole, Robert L. *The Shape and Message of Book III (Psalms 73–89)*. JSOTSup 307. Sheffield, U.K.: Sheffield Academic, 2000.

Craigie, Peter C. *Psalms 1–50*. WBC 19. Waco, Tex.: Word, 1983.

Creach, Jerome F. D. *The Destiny of the Righteous in the Psalms*. St. Louis: Chalice, 2008.

———. *Yahweh as Refuge and the Editing of the Hebrew Psalter*. JSOTSup 217. Sheffield, U.K.: Sheffield Academic, 1996.

Crenshaw, James L. *Defending God: Biblical Responses to the Problem of Evil*. Oxford: Oxford University Press, 2005.

Day, Dorothy. *The Long Loneliness*. New York: Harper & Row, 1952.

DeClaissé-Walford, Nancy L. *Reading from the Beginning: The Shaping of the Hebrew Psalter*. Macon, Ga.: Mercer University Press, 1997.

———, ed. *The Shape and Shaping of the Book of Psalms: The Current State of Scholarship*. AIL 20. Atlanta: Society of Biblical Literature, 2014.

DeClaissé-Walford, Nancy, Rolf A. Jacobson, and Beth LaNeel Tanner. *The Book of Psalms*. NICOT. Grand Rapids: Eerdmans, 2014.

Dillard, Annie. *Teaching a Stone to Talk*. New York: Harper & Row, 1982.

Dobbs-Allsopp, F. W. *On Biblical Poetry*. Oxford: Oxford University Press, 2015.

Fish, Stanley Eugene. *Is There a Text in This Class? The Authority of Interpretive Communities*. Cambridge: Harvard University Press, 1980.

Flint, Peter W. "The Book of Psalms in the Light of the Dead Sea Scrolls." *VT* 48 (1998): 453–72.

———. *The Dead Sea Psalms Scrolls and the Book of Psalms*. STDJ 17. Leiden: Brill, 1997.

Garside, Charles, Jr. "Calvin's Theology of Music: 1536–1543." *Transactions of the American Philosophical Society* 69 (1979): 1–36.

Gerstenberger, Erhard. "Der Psalter als Buch und als Sammlung." In *Neue Wege der Psalmenforschung*, edited by Klaus Seybold and Erich Zenger, 3–13. Herders biblische Studien 1. Freiburg: Herder, 1994.

———. *Psalms: Part 1 with an Introduction to Cultic Poetry*. Vol. 1. FOTL 14. Grand Rapids: Eerdmans, 1988.

Gillingham, Susan E. "Psalmody and Apocalyptic in the Hebrew Bible: Common Vision, Shared Experience?" In *After the Exile: Essays in Honour of Rex Mason*, edited by John Barton and David J. Reimer, 147–69. Macon, Ga.: Mercer University Press, 1996.

———. *Psalms through the Centuries, Volume One*. Blackwell Bible Commentaries. Malden, Mass.: Blackwell, 2008.

———. *Psalms through the Centuries: A Reception History Commentary on Psalms 1–72, Volume Two*. Blackwell Bible Commentaries. Hoboken, N.J.: Wiley & Sons, 2018.

Goldingay, John. *Psalms. Volume 1: Psalms 1–42*. BCOTWP. Grand Rapids: Baker Academic, 2006.

———. *Psalms. Volume 2: Psalms 43–89*. BCOTWP. Grand Rapids: Baker Academic, 2007.

———. *Psalms. Volume 3: Psalms 90–150*. BCOTWP. Grand Rapids: Baker Academic, 2008.

Grant, Jamie A. *The King as Exemplar: The Function of Deuteronomy's Kingship Law in the Shaping of the Book of Psalms.* AcBib 17. Atlanta: Society of Biblical Literature, 2004.

Gunkel, Hermann. *The Psalms: A Form-Critical Introduction.* Translated by Thomas M. Horner. Biblical Series 19. Philadelphia: Fortress, 1967.

Gunkel, Hermann, and Joachim Begrich. *An Introduction to the Psalms: The Genres of the Religious Lyric of Israel.* Translated by James D. Nogalski. Macon, Ga.: Mercer University Press, 1998. German Original 1933.

Harvey, Michael G. "Wittgenstein's Notion of 'Theology as Grammar.'" *RelS* 25 (1989): 89–103.

Holladay, William L. *The Psalms through Three Thousand Years: Prayerbook of a Cloud of Witnesses.* Minneapolis: Fortress, 1993.

Holmer, Paul L. *The Grammar of Faith.* San Francisco: Harper & Row, 1978.

Hopkins, Denise Dombkowski. *Psalms: Books 2–3.* Wisdom Commentary. Collegeville, Minn.: Liturgical Press, 2016.

Hossfeld, Frank-Lothar, and Erich Zenger. *Die Psalmen I: Psalm 1–50.* NEchtB 29. Würzburg: Echter Verlag, 1993.

——. *Psalms 2: A Commentary on Psalms 51–100.* Translated by Linda M. Maloney. Hermeneia. Minneapolis: Fortress, 2005. German Original 2000.

——. *Psalms 3: A Commentary on Psalms 101–150.* Translated by Linda M. Maloney. Hermeneia. Minneapolis: Fortress, 2011. German Original 2008.

Howard, David M. *The Structure of Psalms 93–100.* BJSUCSD 5. Winona Lake, Ind.: Eisenbrauns, 1997.

Jahn, Manfred. "Frames, Preferences, and the Reading of Third Person Narratives: Towards a Cognitive Narratology." *Poetics Today* 18 (1997): 441–68.

Janowski, Bernd. *Arguing with God: A Theological Anthropology of the Psalms.* Translated by Armin Siedlecki. Louisville: Westminster John Knox, 2013.

Johnson, Aubrey R. "The Psalms." In *The Old Testament and Modern Study: A Generation of Discovery and Research: Essays by the Members of the Society,* edited by H. H. Rowley, 162–209. Oxford: Clarendon, 1951.

Koehler, Ludwig, Walter Baumgartner, and Johann Jakob Stamm. *The Hebrew and Aramaic Lexicon of the Old Testament.* Translated and edited under the supervision of M. E. J. Richardson. 5 vols. Leiden: Brill, 1994–2000.

Kraus, Hans-Joachim. *Psalms 60–150: A Commentary.* Translated by Hilton C. Oswald. Minneapolis: Fortress, 1989.

Leuenberger, Martin. *Konzeptionen des Königtums Gottes im Psalter: Untersuchungen zu Komposition und Redaktion der theokratischen Bücher IV–V im Psalter.* ATANT. Zürich: Theologischer, 2004.

Lewis, C. S. *Reflections on the Psalms.* New York: Harcourt Brace, 1958.

Luther, Martin. "Preface to the Psalter." In *Luther's Works,* edited by Helmut T. Lehmann, 253–57. Translated by Charles M. Jacobs. Vol. 35. Philadelphia: Muhlenberg, 1960.

Mandolfo, Carleen. *God in the Dock: Dialogic Tension in the Psalms of Lament.* JSOTSup 357. Sheffield, U.K.: Sheffield Academic, 2002.

Marshall, Molly T. "Plowing the Soil of the Heart: The Psalter and Spirituality." *American Baptist Quarterly* 21 (2002): 499–509.

Mays, James Luther. *The Lord Reigns: A Theological Handbook to the Psalms.* IBC. Louisville: Westminster John Knox, 1994.

McCann, J. Clinton, Jr. "The Book of Psalms." *NIB* 4:639–1280.

———. "Books I–III and the Editorial Purpose of the Hebrew Psalter." In *The Shape and Shaping of the Psalter,* edited by J. Clinton McCann Jr., 93–107. JSOTSup 159. Sheffield, U.K.: JSOT Press, 1993.

———. *A Theological Introduction to the Book of Psalms: The Psalms as Torah.* Nashville: Abingdon, 1993.

Merton, Thomas. *Praying the Psalms.* Collegeville, Minn.: Liturgical Press, 1956.

Millard, Matthias. *Die Komposition des Psalters: ein formgeschichtlicher Ansatz.* FAT 9. Tübingen: J. C. B. Mohr, 1994.

Miller, Patrick D. "The Beginning of the Psalter." In *The Shape and Shaping of the Psalter,* edited by J. Clinton McCann Jr., 83–92. JSOTSup 159. Sheffield, U.K.: JSOT Press, 1993.

Mitchell, David C. *The Message of the Psalter: An Eschatological Programme in the Book of Psalms.* JSOTSup 252. Sheffield, U.K.: Sheffield Academic, 1997.

Moore, Andrew. *Realism and Christian Faith: God, Grammar, and Meaning.* Cambridge: Cambridge University Press, 2003.

Mowinckel, Sigmund. *The Psalms in Israel's Worship.* 2 vols. New York: Abingdon, 1962.

———. "YHWH's Enthronement Festival and the Origin of Eschatology." In Vol. 1 of *Psalm Studies,* 173–491. Translated by Mark E. Biddle. HBS 3. Atlanta: Society of Biblical Literature, 2014. Originally published in *Psalmenstudien vol. 2: Das Thronbesteigungsfest Jahwäs und der Ursprung der Eschatologie.* Repr. Amsterdam: Schippers, 1961.

Nasuti, Harry. *Defining the Sacred Song: Genre, Tradition, and the Post-Critical Interpretation of the Psalms.* JSOTSup 218. Sheffield, U.K.: Sheffield Academic, 1999.

Norris, Kathleen. *The Cloister Walk.* New York: Riverside Books, 1996.

O'Connor, David. "In Defense of Theoretical Theodicy." *Modern Theology* 5 (1988): 61–74.

Parsons, Mikeal C. "Reading a Beginning/Beginning a Reading: Tracing Literary Theory on Narrative Openings." *Semeia* 52 (1990): 11–31.

Penny, Louise. *The Beautiful Mystery.* New York: Minotaur, 2012.

Perry, Menakhem. "Literary Dynamics: How the Order of a Text Creates Its Meanings." *Poetics Today* 1 (1979): 35–64, 311–61.

Pinches, Charles. "Christian Pacifism and Theodicy: The Free Will Defense in the Thought of John H. Yoder." *Modern Theology* 5 (1989): 239–55.

Prince, Gerald. *A Grammar of Stories: An Introduction.* The Hague: Mouton, 1973.

Rechberger, Uwe. *Von der Klage zum Lob. Studien zum "Stimmungsumschwung" in den Psalmen.* WMANT. Neukirchen-Vluyn, Germany: Neukirchener Verlagsgesellschaft, 2012.

Rimmon-Kenan, Shlomith. *Narrative Fiction: Contemporary Poetics.* London: Methuen, 1983.

Said, Edward W. *Beginnings: Intention and Method.* New York: Basic Books, 1975.

Saliers, Don. "Singing Our Lives." In *Practicing Our Faith: A Way of Life for a Searching People,* edited by Dorothy C. Bass, 179–93. San Francisco: Jossey-Bass, 1997.

Sheppard, Gerald T. "Theology and the Book of Psalms." *Int* 46 (1992): 143–55.

Snearly, Michael K. *The Return of the King: Messianic Expectation in Book V of the Psalter.* LHBOTS 624. New York: T&T Clark, 2016.

Surin, Kenneth. "Theodicy?" *HTR* 76 (1983): 225–47.

Tilley, Terence W. *The Evils of Theodicy.* Washington, D.C.: Georgetown University Press, 1991.

Tucker, W. Dennis, Jr. *Constructing and Deconstructing Power in Psalms 107–150.* AIL 19. Atlanta: Society of Biblical Literature, 2014.

———. "Empires and Enemies in Book V of the Psalter." In *The Composition of the Book of Psalms,* edited by Erich Zenger, 723–31. BETL 238. Leuven: Peeters, 2010.

Uspensky, Boris. *A Poetics of Composition: The Structure of the Artistic Text and Typology of a Compositional Form.* Translated by C. Zavarin and S. Wittig. Berkeley: University of California Press, 1973.

Villanueva, Frederico G. *The 'Uncertainty of a Hearing': A Study of the Sudden Change of Mood in the Psalms of Lament.* VTSup. Leiden: Brill, 2008.

Westermann, Claus. *The Living Psalms.* Translated by J. R. Porter. Grand Rapids: Eerdmans, 1989.

———. *Praise and Lament in the Psalms.* Translated by Keith R. Crim and Richard N. Soulen. Atlanta: John Knox, 1981.

———. *The Praise of God in the Psalms.* Richmond: John Knox, 1965.

———. *The Psalms: Structure, Content & Message.* Translated by Ralph D. Gehrke. Minneapolis: Augsburg, 1980.

———. "Zur Sammlung des Psalters." *Theologia Viatorum* 8 (1962): 278–84.

Whybray, R. Norman. *Reading the Psalms as a Book.* JSOTSup 222. Sheffield, U.K.: Sheffield Academic, 1996.

Wiesel, Elie. *The Trial of God.* New York: Schocken Books, 1979.

Willgren, David. *The Formation of the "Book" of Psalms: Reconsidering the Transmission and Canonization of Psalmody in Light of Material Culture and the Poetics of Anthologies.* FAT II 88. Tübingen: Mohr Siebeck, 2016.

Wilson, Gerald Henry. *The Editing of the Hebrew Psalter.* SBLDS 76. Chico, Calif.: Scholars Press, 1985.

———. "A First Century C.E. Date for the Closing of the Book of Psalms?" *JBQ* 28 (2000): 102–10.

Wittgenstein, Ludwig. *Philosophical Investigations.* 3rd ed. Translated by G. E. M. Anscombe. New York: Macmillan, 1968.

Zenger, Erich. "The Composition and Theology of the Fifth Book of Psalms, Psalms 107–145." *JSOT* 80 (1998): 77–102.

———. "Der jüdische Psalter—ein anti-imperiales Buch?" In *Religion und Gesellschaft: Studien zu ihrer Wechselbeziehung in den Kulturen des antiken Vorderen Orients,* edited by Rainer Albertz, 95–108. AZERKAVO 1/AOAT 248. Münster: Ugarit, 1997.

———. "Die Komposition der Wallfahrtpsalmen Ps 120–134: Zum Program der Psalterexegese." In *Paradigmen auf dem Prüfstand: Exegese wider den Strich,* edited by Martin Ebner and Bernhard Heininger, 173–90. Münster: Aschendorff, 2004.

———. *A God of Vengeance? Understanding the Psalms of Divine Wrath.* Louisville: Westminster John Knox, 1996.

AUTHOR AND SUBJECT INDEX

Adams, Kevin, 112n30
Alter, Robert, 56, 117n7, 122n23
ancient Israel, 4, 9, 11, 13, 28–31, 41–42,
    47, 53, 58, 65, 83, 103; covenant, 31;
    defeats, 31; the exodus traditions of,
    53; experience of exile, 83; the faith
    community of, 58; the hymnbook of
    the faith community of, 5; history, 33,
    53; regular and festival worship, 10;
    salvation history, 25, 31, 59; social
    and religious life, 9, 15; worship, 10,
    62; in Zion, 57
Anderson, Bernhard W., 23, 115n3
Anderson, George W., 67, 118n21
Asaphite collection, 11–12, 70, 81, 101
'ašrê, 64, 76
Athanasius, 2, 111n8
Augustine, 2–3, 111n9, 115n8

Babylonian exile, the, 13, 60, 104
Ballhorn, Egbert, 97, 107, 109, 122n20,
    122n22, 122n23, 122n24, 122n25,
    123n51, 124n57
Begrich, Joachim, 26–27, 94, 113n43,
    115n10, 117n2, 124n55, 124n56
Bell, Richard H., 113n36
Bellinger, W. H., Jr., 113n42, 113n46,

114n59, 114n61, 114n64, 115n9,
115n14, 115n15, 116n17, 116n18,
116n25, 116n33, 116n35, 116n38,
116n40, 116n42, 116n43, 116n44,
117n8, 117n10, 117n13, 117n46,
118n1, 118n18, 118n20, 119n28,
120n39, 120n41, 120n44, 120n45,
120n46, 120n51, 120n53, 120n54,
120n56, 121n5, 121n59, 122n16,
122n17, 122n27, 123n31, 123n36,
123n46, 123n49
ben-'ādām, 20
Benedictine Rule, the, 2
Blumenthal, David R., 32, 116n19
Bonhoeffer, Dietrich, 4, 122n24
Book of Praises, 7–8, 97
books of Samuel, 11
Book I (Pss 1–41), 42, 49, 61,
    75–77, 96–97
Books I–II (Pss 1–72), 28, 34, 38, 80, 89,
    96, 102, 109
Books I–III (Pss 1–89), 13, 70, 92–93
Book II (Pss 42–72), 31, 33, 36–37,
    61–62, 78–79, 80–81, 96, 100
Book III (Pss 73–89), 13–14, 29, 32, 56,
    59, 65, 71–72, 78–79, 80–83, 87–89,
    93, 96, 98, 100–102, 108–9

Book IV (Pss 90–106), 13–14, 58–59, 65, 71, 82–84, 87–89, 93, 96, 98–102, 109

Books IV–V (Pss 90–150), 13, 66, 70–72, 88–89, 92, 95–98, 100, 108

Book V, 13, 52, 71, 84–86, 88–89, 91, 94, 96, 97, 99–100, 102–9, 119n27, 124n54

Brown, William P., 15, 114n54, 114n55, 114n56, 116n39, 120n40, 120n47, 120n52

Brueggemann, Walter, 11–12, 49, 71, 76, 93, 112n27, 113n47, 114n51, 114n61, 114n64, 115n14, 115n15, 116n17, 116n18, 116n33, 116n35, 116n38, 116n40, 116n42, 116n43, 116n44, 117n46, 117n49, 117n10, 117n13, 118n12, 118n18, 118n20, 120n33, 120n39, 120n44, 120n45, 120n46, 120n51, 120n53, 120n54, 120n56, 121n9, 122n27, 123n46, 123n49

Buber, Martin, 117n10

Buss, Martin J., 94, 122n14

Buttrick, George Arthur, 115n4

Calvin, John, 3, 112n15, 112n16, 112n18, 115n8

Candler, Peter M., Jr., 7, 113n7

Childs, Brevard S., 70, 76, 92, 115n7, 118n2, 120n31, 121n6

Clifford, Richard J., 114n58, 114n62, 114n65, 116n26, 116n30, 116n35, 117n5, 117n45

Cole, Robert L., 89, 100, 121n62, 122n28

Craigie, Peter C., 115n16

Creach, Jerome F. D., 13, 71, 77, 114n51, 118n13, 120n37

creator (referring to God or YHWH), 9–10, 13, 19–21, 23, 29, 33, 48, 51, 57–58, 60, 62, 79, 83, 103, 107–8

Crenshaw, James L., 102, 123n33

dāmâ, 62

Davidic collection, 11–12, 37, 66, 70, 78, 85, 92, 104–7

Davidic dynasty, 71

Davidic kingdom, 13, 32, 59, 65, 83, 86–87, 89, 92, 96, 98, 100–101

Davidic psalms, 11–12, 79, 96

Day of Atonement, 59

Day, Dorothy, 3, 112n21

Dead Sea Scrolls: *see* Qumran community; Qumran material

DeClaissé-Walford, Nancy L., 70, 76, 85, 113n50, 114n59, 114n60, 114n63, 116n20, 116n24, 116n27, 116n29, 116n34, 116n35, 116n36, 116n40, 117n3, 117n5, 117n6, 117n11, 118n7, 120n35, 120n43, 120n48, 120n49, 120n55, 120n57, 121n8, 123n29

dialogue, 33, 35, 47, 73, 97, 99, 102; covenant, 31, 77, 90; with the emphasis on the shape of the book of Psalms, 15; of faith, 11, 45, 47, 63, 66, 89, 101–2; between the faith community and YHWH, 100; interfaith, 4; between Israel and YHWH, 89; with the reality of exile, 87; with YHWH, 87

die Gewissheit der Erhörung, 93

Dillard, Annie, 61, 118n16

divine presence, the, 18, 39, 50, 53, 62, 79–82, 96, 106; the blessing of, 77; the place of, 30, 62; a sacred place of, 78; special, 29

Dobbs-Allsopp, F. W., 114n54

early church fathers and mothers, 2

Egyptian Hallel, 52, 103

Elohistic Psalter (Pss 42–83), 11, 79, 81, 115n13

'emet, 53, 81

'ĕnôš, 20

Enthronement Psalm(s), 59–60, 70, 83, 88, 93, 100

fall of Jerusalem, 13, 28–29, 31, 46, 66, 87, 89, 92, 96, 100, 102, 108–9

Feast of Tabernacles, 60

Fish, Stanley Eugene, 119n22

Flint, Peter W., 73, 119n20

form critics, 27, 94

SCRIPTURE INDEX